Joanna Hooe Mathews

Bessie Among the Mountains

Joanna Hooe Mathews

Bessie Among the Mountains

ISBN/EAN: 9783337289713

Printed in Europe, USA, Canada, Australia, Japan

Cover: Foto ©ninafisch / pixelio.de

More available books at **www.hansebooks.com**

BESSIE AMONG THE MOUNTAINS.

BOOKS BY JOANNA H. MATHEWS.

I. THE BESSIE BOOKS.
6 vols. In a box. $7.50.

II. THE FLOWERETS.
A SERIES OF STORIES ON THE COMMANDMENTS.
6 vols. In a box. $3.60.

III. LITTLE SUNBEAMS.
6 vols. In a box. $6.00.

IV. KITTY AND LULU BOOKS.
6 vols. In a box. $6.00.

V. MISS ASHTON'S GIRLS.
6 vols. In a neat box. $7.50.

VI. HAPS AND MISHAPS.
6 vols. $7.50.

BY JULIA A. MATHEWS.

I. DARE TO DO RIGHT SERIES.
5 vols. In a box. $5.50.

II. DRAYTON HALL STORIES.
Illustrative of the Beatitudes. 6 vols. In a box. $4.50.

III. THE GOLDEN LADDER SERIES.
Stories illustrative of the Lord's Prayer. 6 vols. $3.00.

ROBERT CARTER AND BROTHERS,

New York.

Bessie among the Mountains.

FRONTISPIECE.

BESSIE

AMONG

THE MOUNTAINS.

BY

JOANNA H. MATHEWS,

AUTHOR OF "BESSIE AT THE SEASIDE," "BESSIE IN THE CITY," AND
"BESSIE AND HER FRIENDS."

"Be not overcome of evil, but overcome evil with good."

NEW YORK:
ROBERT CARTER AND BROTHERS,
530, BROADWAY.

Entered according to Act of Congress, in the year 1869, by

ROBERT CARTER AND BROTHERS,

In the Clerk's Office of the District Court of the United States for the Southern District of New York.

CAMBRIDGE:
PRESS OF JOHN WILSON AND SON.

TO

RICHARD HOWLAND HUNT,

The Dear Little Boy,

WHO "NEARLY KNOWS HOW TO READ, AND THINKS COUSIN JOSIE'S STORIES HAVE NOT A BIT OF STUPIDNESS IN THEM."

CONTENTS.

Chapter		Page.
I.	Up the Mountain	9
II.	The Squirrels and the Ice Glen	33
III.	A Visit to Aunt Patty	55
IV.	Lem and Dolly	74
V.	The Gardens	98
VI.	The Sunday School	113
VII.	The Silver Cup	128
VIII.	A Kind Word for Lem	147
IX.	Dol's Revenge	163
X.	The Bananas	183
XI.	"Good for Evil"	203
XII.	Uncle Ruthven's Work	220
XIII.	A Ride on the Sheaves	236
XIV.	Blackberrying	255
XV.	A Friend in Need	276
XVI.	Lem's Sorrow	299
XVII.	Dolly Goes Home	317
XVIII.	Good-by to Chalecoo	336

BESSIE AMONG THE MOUNTAINS.

I.

UP THE MOUNTAIN.

UP, up! What a height it was, and how the horses toiled as they drew the heavy wagons up the mountain side. Whenever they came to a very steep place, the boys and all the gentlemen, except Colonel Rush, would jump out and walk, so as to lighten the load. Aunt Annie and Aunt Bessie, who was really Aunt Bessie now, for she was Uncle Ruthven's wife, also tried this; but they soon tired, and were glad to take their seats in the wagon again.

Maggie thought she must take her turn too, and asked papa to lift her out. Papa consented, warning her, however, that she would find it harder work than she imagined to clamber up these steep ascents on her own two small feet. But Maggie thought she would like to be "a relief to the horses," so papa took her out.

Then Bessie's sweet little voice piped up from the snug corner, where she sat nestled between Colonel Rush and his wife.

"Mamma, bettn't I walk a little too, on 'count of the poor horses?"

At which Mr. Porter who walked beside the wagon, holding the reins, and now and then chirruping to the willing creatures who needed no whip or harsh command, turned his head towards the tiny figure with a merry twinkle in his eye.

"I think not, darling," said mamma; "by the time we are at the Lake House you will be more than tired enough with this long day's journey."

"I do not wish to walk, mamma," said Bessie, "only for the horses."

"The horses don't make much account of

your weight, I reckon," said Mr. Porter, good naturedly, "and though this seems mighty hard work to you, they are used to it, and don't mind it so much. Besides, they know that every pitch takes them nearer to their stable, where they'll have a good rest and a feed of oats. They'd rather go up than down any day."

"How do they know it?" asked Bessie, who had already made friends with Mr. Porter.

"Well," said Mr. Porter, taking off his hat and fanning himself with it, "I can't just say how; certain it is they do know it."

"Maybe it's their instinct," said Bessie.

"That's about it," he answered, with a smile.

"These are fine teams of yours, Mr. Porter," said Colonel Rush.

"You may say that, sir," answered the old man, looking with pride at the noble beasts, "and this is the best of the lot. These are Vermont horses, sure-footed as goats, as they need to be on these mountain roads; strong as elephants, and wiser than many a creature that goes on two feet. Why, I could tell you stories of this fellow," and he nodded towards the horse nearest him, "that maybe you'll find it hard to believe. I named him 'Solomon,' thinking it suitable; but the boys they shortened it to 'Sol,' and that's what he goes by. I tell you, he knows a thing or two, that horse."

Mr. Porter paused for breath, and Bessie, after waiting a moment or two in hopes of the stories of old Sol, said, —

"We'll believe you, Mr. Porter, if you tell us those stories."

"So I will," he answered, "but not now. It takes the breath out of a man trudging up these hills, and I can't tell you long stories now. But you come into the kitchen some evening, and I'll tell you a bushel full."

Maggie had found that "trudging up the hills" took the breath out of a little girl, and papa's words soon proved themselves true; but she plodded along perseveringly, flushed and panting, holding to papa's hand, and happy in her belief that she was sparing the horses by her own exertions.

And now they came to a level spot where all might rest. A beautiful resting place it was, a perfect bower of the wild clematis, rock ivy and briar rose, the latter now in full flower. The long, slender sprays flung themselves from tree to tree, or ran climbing over the rocks, while the delicate pink blossoms hung, many of them, within the children's reach. Uncle Ruthven's warning checked Maggie's too eager fingers until he could cut them carefully with his knife, and place them in her hands stripped of their sharp little thorns. Maggie thanked him for his thoughtful kindness when she saw the misfortune which had happened to Hafed; for the little Persian, always anxious to please his " Missys," had grasped too heedlessly the tempting branches, and was now wringing his fingers as he danced about, half laughing, half crying, and saying, —

"Prettys no good, no good."

Maggie and Bessie were quite distressed for him, until his master, having taken out the thorns, bade him wash his bleeding fingers in the brook which ran by the roadside. Bessie had been taken from the wagon that she might rest herself by running about a little after her long ride, and now she and Maggie, as well as Hafed, forgot pricks and scratches in the pleasure of watching the brook, and feeling its cool, clear waters trickle through their fingers. What a noisy, merry, frolicksome stream this was, gurgling and splashing, rushing and tumbling in its rocky bed; now leaping gracefully in a miniature waterfall over some narrow ledge, now rippling and singing about the roots of the trees and over the pebbles that lay in its course, now flashing in the sunlight, and now hiding in a crevice of the rocks as if it were playing at Bopeep.

"What a fuss it makes about nothing," said Harry, as he dipped his fingers into the water, and carried some of the clear, sparkling drops to his lips, "One would think it was doing a wonderful lot of work."

"So it does," said Maggie, following her brother's example.

"What work does it do?" asked Harry, always ready to listen to any of Maggie's new ideas.

"Sometimes it gives a thirsty boy a drink, and he is very ungrateful, and says it makes a fuss about nothing," said Maggie, mischievously.

Harry playfully sprinkled her with the drops which hung from his fingers. "And what else?"

"It waters the flowers and mosses and trees," said Maggie; "and the birds and squirrels can come and take a drink too, if they like."

"And it makes a pretty waterfall for us to see, and a nice, pleasant noise for us to listen to," said Bessie.

"All that is no better than play," said Harry.

"And it helps to make the sea," said Bessie. "Mamma said so."

"Ho!" said Fred; "much this little brook does towards filling the sea, Queen Bess."

"But *it helps*, and does all it can, Fred."

"Yes," said Maggie; "one little brook runs on until it finds another little brook, and then they join, and run on together, and then they meet another and another till they all make a small river, and that joins other little rivers and brooks, till there is a very large one like that we sailed on this morning, and that runs into the great, great sea that we used to see at Quam Beach last summer."

"Hallo, Midge!" said Fred; "where did you find out so much?"

"It's not my own finding out," said Maggie; "the other day my geography lesson was about rivers, and mamma told me all that, and Bessie heard too; so when we first saw this brook farther down the mountain, we remembered what mamma said, and Aunt May said a very nice thing."

"What was it?" asked Harry.

"She said little children might be like the brooks and springs. Not one could do a great deal by himself, but every little helped in the work God gave his creatures to do for him, just as every brook helped to fill the great sea to which it ran; and if we were good and sweet, it made everything bright and pleasant about us, just like a clear and running stream. But cross and naughty children were like the muddy brooks and dull pools, which no one could drink, or make of any use. I hope I wont be like an ugly, muddy pool that does no good to any one, but just stands still, and looks disagreeable all the day long, and has toads and things in it."

The boys laughed at the ending of Maggie's speech, so like herself, and Uncle Ruthven as he dipped a drinking cup into the flashing stream, said, —

"I do not think we need fear that, little Maggie."

"No," said Harry; "there is rather too

much sunshine and sparkle about Maggie to think that she would become a stagnant pool, full of ugly tempers and hateful faults, like 'toads and things.'"

"Yes," laughed Fred, "and she could not stand still with nothing to do; could you, Midget Fidget?"

Maggie was in too sunny a humor to be teased by anything Fred could say, though she did not like the name he called her, and she answered with good temper,—

"No, indeed, I could not, Fred; but if I am naughty I suppose I do not run just the way I ought to, and perhaps I grow a little muddy sometimes."

"It don't last long then, I'll say that for you," answered Fred, touched by his little sister's sweet-tempered honesty.

"No, it does not," said Bessie, who had been listening to the last few sentences with a sober face, "and my own little brook Maggie is the best and brightest brook of all the family. No, thank you, Uncle Ruthven," as her uncle offered her a drink from his cup; "the water tastes better this way;" and she dipped her tiny hand again in the stream.

"But it would take you till sundown to satisfy your thirst out of that make-believe hand, Princess," said Mr. Stanton, "and Mr. Porter is ready for a fresh start."

So Bessie took a drink from her uncle's cup, and the other children were glad to do the same, since they were now forced to leave this pleasant spot.

Mamma said she thought Maggie had walked far enough, so she once more took her seat in the wagon, and as Mr. Porter said they had passed the steepest part of the ascent, the gentlemen and boys all did the same. The scene did not grow less beautiful as they went on upward. They could see to a great distance, and the view was very lovely. Behind and below them lay hills and forests, with here and there a break or clearing where some cozy home farm nestled, with the smoke from its chimney curling lazily up into the quiet summer air. Still farther down, the valleys with their glistening ponds and streams, and the villages clustering here and there, their houses and churches looking from this height almost as small as toys; while far in the distance, flashing in the sunlight, rolled the noble river up whose waters they had come that morning.

Around them and above them lay great swells of land, over which they had yet to pass, rising one above another till they were crowned with the lofty summit of the mountain. Here stood out sharply against the sky a gray, bare mass of rock, with a tuft of pine-trees growing on the very top. By some people this was called "The Point," by others, "The Chief's Head," because they fancied it looked like an Indian's head wearing a plume of feathers. It could be seen for many miles, and long before our party began to ascend the mountain, Mr. Bradford had pointed it out to the children. The boys at once imagined they saw the Indian's head plainly. Maggie sometimes thought she did, sometimes thought she did not, and was very eager about it; but now as the road took a sudden bend, bringing the great rock into nearer view, she declared the likeness was to be seen distinctly, nose, mouth, chin and all.

Bessie could not see any resemblance, and since Maggie could, was rather distressed; but mamma and the Colonel consoled her by saying that they, like herself, could see nothing but a huge, gray stone, crowned by a few lonely-looking trees.

"There's more fancy than anything else about it, I believe myself," said Mr. Porter; "if it was not for the old story probably no one would see any resemblance."

"What story?" asked Harry, eagerly.

"Why," answered Mr. Porter, " it is said that a tribe of Indians once lived among these valleys and mountains, whose chief died. He left twin sons, both famous warriors, and it was doubtful which would be chosen by the tribe to be their chief or king in the father's place. One of the brothers was very anxious for this honor. He was a proud and selfish man, who seemed to care for no one in the world but his beautiful young wife, whom he dearly loved. His brother was more of a favorite with the people, and he feared that their choice would fall upon him, so he determined to kill him that he might be out of his way.

"The brother was fond of climbing to the mountain top, and sitting there to look out over the broad lands which had belonged to his fathers for so many years. One night when the wicked chief was returning from the hunt, he saw, as he thought, in the dim moonlight, his brother sitting in his usual place. This was very near the edge of the rock, where a slight push might throw him over, and it came into the bad man's heart to climb up softly behind him, and, with a sudden shove, to send him down upon the rocks below. He gave himself no time to think, and in a few moments he had reached the quiet figure which was half concealed by a clump of trees, and, with a push of his powerful hand, sent it whirling over into the valley below."

"Oh, the bad, bad man!" said Bessie. "He was just like a Cain, and his poor brother who never did him any harm! I think that is a bad story."

"Probably it's not true, but just a fable," said Mr. Porter.

"Then they oughtn't to say it about the poor Indian," said Bessie, indignantly. "If he didn't do it, they ought not to make it up about him."

"And likely enough the man himself never lived," said Mr. Porter.

"Then they oughtn't to say he did," persisted Bessie; "And to make him so wicked too. There's enough of bad people without making up any more."

"Well, what was the end of it?" asked Fred.

"Just as the poor lost one went over the edge, a scream rang out on the night air, and the Indian knew it was the voice of his beloved wife whom he had thus sent to her death. The story goes on to say that he was so stricken with horror and grief when he found what he had done, that he wished the earth might open and swallow him, which it did, all but his head, which was turned into stone, and so has remained to speak of the punishment of his wicked deed."

"That tribe of Indians must have been giants then," said Harry, laughing as he looked up at the enormous mass of stone.

"Now I know that story never was," said Bessie. "People don't be turned into stone because they are bad, and nobody ever had such a big head, and people ought not to say it."

Bessie had heard many a fairy tale, many a fable, and had never objected to them, though she always preferred to listen to stories which were, or might be, true; but somehow, no one could tell why, this fancy about the rock seemed to shock her sense of truth, and from this time she could never be persuaded to call it the "Chief's Head." Her mother also noticed that when she was out of doors, she always sat or stood with her back towards it if she could possibly do so.

But they were by no means to mount so far as this before they came to their resting-place. Chalecoo Lake lay a good way below the "Point," nestled in a beautiful basin among the hills, and here the road ended. Those who wished to go higher must do so by a rough mountain path which led to the very summit.

The children were delighted to see what a quantity of birds and squirrels there appeared to be in the woods. The former were hopping about all over the trees, singing among the branches, and seeming scarcely disturbed by the approach of the wagons.

As for the squirrels, they were as saucy as possible, waiting and watching with their sharp, bright eyes till the travellers were close upon them, then gliding ahead to a short distance and looking back, or perhaps leaping from one to another of the old fallen trunks which lay by the roadside almost within arm's length.

Once as the party, who were all growing somewhat tired, were rather quiet, they suddenly heard a long, loud chirrup; and looking round to the side whence the noise came, there, upon a heap of stones, sat a large gray squirrel, with his tail curled gracefully over his back like a plume, and seeming to call attention to himself by his song. Not in the least alarmed by the eager delight of the children, or the whistling and shouts of the boys, he sat still till all the wagons had passed, when he darted ahead of the foremost one, and seating himself this time on an old rail fence, began his pretty call again, and took a second close look at our friends. This he did five or six times in succession, to the great amusement and satisfaction of the little ones, who were beginning to hope he would go with them all the way to the house, when with a pert, defiant whisk of his bushy tail, he leaped down the bank, and was lost to sight in the thick trees of the ravine.

At another time a rabbit ran across the road, but he was by no means so sociable as Bunny, and scampered away as if his life depended on hiding himself among the bushes as fast as possible.

"You wait till to-morrow morning," said Mr. Porter, as Bessie said how sorry she was that the squirrel had not kept on with them; "You wait till to-morrow morning and you'll see squirrels enough for the asking. Tame as your little dog there, they are too."

"Oh, Mr. Porter!" said Bessie, "do you shut the poor little squirrels up in a cage?"

"Not I," answered Mr. Porter. "I would not allow it on any account, and never did. You'll see how my boy Bob manages them."

And now they came to the lake itself. What a wild, curious place it was, such as none of the children had ever seen, not even Harry, who was considered by his brothers and sisters quite a travelled young gentle man, because he had at one time gone with his father to Washington, and at another to Niagara.

Great masses and blocks of granite lay piled one above another round three sides of the lake, here and there poised in such a manner that many of them looked as if the slightest touch must send them headlong into the waters below. And yet thus they had remained for hundreds, perhaps thousands of years, held firmly by the Almighty Hand which had given to each its place. Mosses and lichens, of all shades of gray, green and brown, covered their weather-beaten sides, while their tops were crowned with oaks, maples, pines and firs.

Around the southern side, and close to the mountain, which here rose still farther up, up, steep and rugged, to the Point, or Indian's Head, wound the road; and a dangerous road it looked, with the deep waters of the lake on one side, the rough mountain on the other where the huge boulders overhung the travellers as they passed on. But with surefooted, steady horses, and a careful driver, Mr. Bradford said there was no danger, for the road was good and strong, "built upon a rock," and kept in capital order by Mr. Porter and his industrious sons. Still, more than one of the ladies drew a breath of relief when it was safely passed.

Away at the eastern end, where there was a break in the rock, and a little back from the lake, stood Mr. Porter's house, a long, low, pleasant-looking building, painted white, with green blinds, wide piazzas, and magnificent shade trees. Garden, orchard and fields lay behind on the slope of the hill where it fell gently away to the valley below, and the whole place told of order and industry, showing in beautiful contrast to the wild grandeur of the other sides of the lake.

So here Maggie and Bessie were at last, at the long-talked-of Chalecoo Lake; and glad enough they, as well as the rest of the party, were to be at their journey's end, pleasant though it had been. Ten hours of steady travelling was tiresome work for little people.

In the wide-open doorway stood Mrs. Porter, waiting to welcome them.

"What a jolly-looking old lady!" exclaimed Fred. "I shall like her, I know. She looks as if she belonged to this dear old place."

"That's so," said Mr. Porter, putting his head on one side, and gazing admiringly at his wife; "She's as jolly as she looks, and as good as she's jolly. My! but she'll spoil your children, Mrs. Bradford."

Mrs. Bradford smiled, and did not look as if she thought the "spoiling" would hurt her children very much; and now, with a loud "whoa," Mr. Porter drew in his horses, and his wife with her two daughters came down to help unload.

"You see I have brought you a large family, Mrs. Porter," said Mrs. Bradford, "but you have room for all, I believe?"

"Yes, and heart room too," was the answer, as the old lady took baby from her nurse, and covered her with kisses. Miss Baby looked for a moment as if she had half a mind to resent this liberty, but thought better of it, and presently was crowing and smiling in the kind old face, which looked so pleasantly at her. Indeed, not one of the children could resist the cheery, coaxing voice and tender manner; and in five minutes they were all crowding about her, as she told of all the treats she had in store for them; and even shy Maggie had summoned up courage to ask a question which had long been troubling her.

"Mrs. Porter," she whispered, pulling the old lady's head down towards her, "may I ask you a secret?"

"To be sure, my lamb, a dozen if you like," answered Mrs. Porter.

"Do you have trundle beds?" whispered Maggie again.

"Trundle beds? Well, I believe there is

an old one up garret," said Mrs. Porter, " but I'll have it down for you, and put to rights if you like."

"Oh, no!" said Maggie, "please don't. I *do hate* them so, and I had to sleep in one all last summer at Quam."

"Oh! that's it," said Mrs. Porter, "well, you shall sleep in no trundle bed here, since you don't like it. Come along up-stairs, and you shall see what nice little cottage beds we have for you young ones."

So this trouble was at an end, and Maggie felt quite free to enjoy all the new pleasures about her, without fear of the dreaded trundle bed.

II.

THE SQUIRRELS AND THE ICE GLEN.

MAGGIE would have liked very well to run about a little on that first evening of their arrival at Chalecoo; but Bessie was so tired that her mother wished her to keep quiet; and as Maggie would not go out without her sister, they both contented themselves with making acquaintance with the house and the people who belonged there. And a delightful house it was to make acquaintance with, — full of all kinds of odd nooks and corners, with two or three steps here leading up to one room, two or three there going down to another; queer little pantries and cupboards and crooked passages, and altogether unlike any other house the children had ever seen. Through the centre was a wide, cool hall with a green blind door at either end, a capital place for a play-room on a rainy day; and around three sides ran a broad piazza, well shaded with vines and the noble old trees among which the house stood.

From the front, one looked out upon the lake and rocks; from the back, far away over hill and valley, mountain and river. Green fields and meadows lay below, with here and there an orchard or a lovely piece of woods. Then the rooms were so large and pleasant, with so many doors and windows that not a breath of air could stir but a breeze must sweep through them, while nothing could be more neat, clean and fresh. Not a speck or spot was to be seen anywhere, not a thing was out of place, and Bessie looking gravely about her as she noticed these signs of care, said anxiously to Mrs. Porter,

"Are you very particular about your nice house, ma'am?"

"Well, yes," answered Mrs. Porter, looking

around with an air of some pride and satisfaction, " don't it suit you?"

"Oh! yes, ma'am," said Bessie, " it suits me very much, but you know sometimes children make a little disorder when they play, and I only meant would you mind if we mussed up your nice house just a very little bit?"

"Not I," said Mrs. Porter, "there's plenty of hands to set to rights any disorder you may make. Just you play away and don't trouble your head about that."

The measure of Maggie's content was full when she followed the old lady up stairs and saw the two neat, small, white beds intended for Bessie and herself.

"Bessie," she said, a little later, "don't you think this place is nicer than Quam Beach?"

They were standing together in the lower hall, looking out upon the lake, while the rays of the setting sun came flickering through the vine leaves, and dancing over the two little figures standing in the doorway, as if it were bidding them a friendly good night, and giving them a promise of a fair day for to-morrow's rambles.

"I think it is very nice," answered Bessie.

"But don't you think it *nicer* than Quam, Bessie?"

"No, Maggie, for the sea is not here."

"But the lake is," said Maggie.

"But the lake is not the sea," said Bessie.

Maggie could not contradict this, but she did not feel satisfied that Bessie should not be as well pleased as she was herself, and she said wistfully, —

"But don't you think you could be a little contented here, Bessie?"

"I can be much contented here, Maggie," answered the little girl. "Why, dear, do you think I would be so ungrateful of this very nice place, and the kind people that are here as not to be contented? Oh! I like the mountains very much, but not quite so very much as the sea."

"Oh, ho!" said Mr. Porter, who had just

come up behind them and heard what Bessie had said last, "so you do not like the mountains as well as the sea? Well, I shall make you change that tune. Why, you don't know all the things there are to see here. Before you've been here a week you'll tell me you like the mountains a heap better than the ocean."

But Mr. Porter was mistaken. He never heard Bessie say that. She spent a very happy summer, and was well satisfied with all the new pleasures she found among the mountains, but they never could make her forget her beloved sea, nor could the old gentleman persuade her to acknowledge that she liked the one as well as the other.

Bessie might well say they were nice people in this house. Besides Mr. and Mrs. Porter, who have already been introduced, were their five sons, "the boys," Mr. Porter called them. Queer "boys," Maggie and Bessie thought them; all, save the youngest, great, sturdy men with sunburned faces and toil-hardened hands. But though their hands were hard, their hearts were not, and seemed to have a particularly soft spot for all these little ones. Mr. Porter's family were all fond of children, and never seemed to think anything too much trouble which could possibly give them pleasure. Next to these grown up "boys," came Fanny and Dolly, two lively, good natured young women; and last of all, Bob, a boy about fourteen, quite ready to make friends with the children, and to show them all the wonders of the place.

The first thing to be thought of after breakfast the next morning was the squirrels. Bob was as anxious to show them to the little strangers as they were to see them; and followed by the whole troop, he led the way to their haunt. This was a great black-walnut tree, which stood at a short distance from the house, and threw its green branches far and wide, casting a delightful shade below, and furnishing a cosy home and leafy play-ground for the squirrels. About half way up the trunk was a hole which was the entrance to their nest. At this hour of the day, Mr. and Mrs. Bunny and their family were generally to be seen frisking about all over and among the boughs, waiting for the nice breakfast which was sure to be provided for them by the kind young master who had chosen them for his pets. If the squirrels could have reasoned about it, they would probably have said that Bob Porter was a capital master to belong to. He fed them and played with them, never shutting them up or asking any work in return; their love was all he wanted, and that he had gained in a way curious to see.

They were usually ready enough to welcome his approach; but now, startled by the unaccustomed sight of so many strangers, every mother's son and daughter of them scampered away to hide themselves in the nest. In half a moment not the end of a tail or the tip of a nose was to be seen, and the children feared that they were to be disappointed.

But telling them to stand at a little distance from him, yet not so far but that they could see all that passed, Bob sat down upon the end of a log and began calling gently, "Bunny, Bunny."

Presently a black nose, two cute little ears, and a pair of sharp, bright eyes appeared at the opening in the tree. The nose sniffed about in a very suspicious manner, and the eyes wandered from Bob to the group beyond, and then back again to Bob, as if they would ask, "Who are all these strange people? Are they friends or foes? and why have you brought them here?"

But at last, as if satisfied that the new faces were friendly ones, Papa Squirrel, for it was he, put forth his whole head, next his gray body appeared, and then his beautiful, feathery tail. Running along a branch he curved his tail over his head, and sitting down, gave a cheerful, chirruping call, which perhaps meant that there was no danger; for in a moment the whole tree seemed to be alive with the rest of the family. Eleven squirrels in all, large and small, were counted by the delighted children. But although they watched their young visitors from among the branches they still seemed too timid to come nearer and take the tempting breakfast which Bob had provided for them; till Mrs. Bunny, either more hungry or less cautious than her mate and children, came whisking down the trunk of the walnut-tree, and in another moment was seated upon Bob's shoulder, holding in her fore-paws the almond he had given her, and opening it with her sharp, pointed teeth. This was too much for the others, and one after another they descended the tree and received their breakfast. There sat Bob, a squirrel upon each shoulder, one on his head, others on his knees and hands, while one little fellow perched upon the toe of his boot, and, with a very contented air cracked and eat his almond.

It was a pretty sight, and a proud boy was Bob, as he sat thus surrounded by his pets, and listened to the exclamations of delight and wonder uttered by the other children in a low tone, lest they should again startle the little creatures. They were particularly amused by the antics of one saucy rogue, who, not satisfied with the share which had fallen to him, crept under Bob's arm, and actually began thrusting his nose into his pocket in search of more almonds. Not finding any, he became indignant, and raced off to the tree, where he seated himself on the end of a bough, and chattered away as though he were scolding at Bob for not having provided more.

"He is the greedy one of the lot," said Bob, "and I have to watch him, or he eats his own share and then robs those that are weaker than himself, if he gets the chance."

"But how did you do it, Bob?" asked Harry. "How did you tame them so when they were not in a cage?"

"Oh! it's not so hard," said Bob, a little boastfully. "You see father will never let me shut up any animal or any bird that is used to being free; and I was set upon having a tame squirrel. This old fellow here," and Bob pointed to the largest of the squirrels which sat upon his shoulder; " this old fellow and his mate lived in the walnut, and I was wild to catch them. But, as father said no, I thought I would hit upon a plan by which they would learn to know me, and come at my call. So one day I left two nuts here on the log, and went away. When I came back some time after, the nuts were gone. This I did the next day and the next, always keeping about for a while first. Then I put down the nuts and went off yonder to that maple, where I waited. It's not so far but that the squirrels could see me, but after watching me for a few moments as if they thought I might be laying a trap for them, they whisked down after the nuts, and then whisked back again in a terrible hurry. Every day I came a little nearer than the day before, and they soon learned to know me; I could even see that they watched for me. At last one day I laid a couple of almonds on one end of the log, and sat down on the other. It was a good while before they would come down that day, but at last they did, and after that I had no more trouble. When they found I did not try to touch them, they came nearer and nearer, till at last they took the nuts from my hand, and now as you see, they are as tame as squirrels could be, and have taught their young ones to have no fear of me. It is two years this summer since I tamed the old pair, and now the rest all know me as well as they do."

"It's jolly fun to see them," said Fred.

"And it's a great deal jolly funnier than if you caught them and shut them up in a cage, is it not?" said Bessie.

The boys laughed.

"Yes, indeed," answered Bob. "Hi, hi! what ails the fellows?" as all the squirrels sprang from him and whisked up the walnut tree. What "ailed the fellows," was soon seen, for even as he spoke, Flossy, who had been left shut up in the house lest he should frighten the bunnies, came tearing round a great rock, and rushed to the foot of the tree, where he commenced a great barking. But the squirrels were all safe in their green house, and as if they knew this, peeped down from among the leaves at Flossy with the greatest unconcern.

Flossy was followed by papa, Uncle Ruthven and the Colonel; and Uncle Ruthven confessed himself the guilty person who had let Flossy escape out of his prison.

"The poor fellow thought it hard he should not have his share of fun, and was making a pitiful whining and whimpering," said Mr. Stanton, "so I let him out on the promise that he should be good."

"But how could he promise when he can't speak?" said Bessie.

"I asked him if he would be quiet and good like a well brought up puppy if I let him out, and he said 'wow,' which in dog language means yes, does it not?" asked Uncle Ruthven.

"And it means no, and thank you, and if you please, and I love you, and everything else he wants to say," said Maggie, catching up her frisky pet in her arms and giving him a hug, which he returned by putting his cold nose in her face, after which he struggled to be put down again, for so glad was he to be free this pleasant morning that he wished to show it by frolicking about on his own four feet.

And now papa proposed they should visit the Ice Glen, to which the children, who had had enough of the squirrels for the present, readily agreed. This Ice Glen was a very wonderful place, interesting even to grown people, and the whole party were anxious to visit it; so they stopped at the house that mamma and the other ladies might join them. The last part of the walk was rather rough, and it was as much as the Colonel, with the help of his cane and Mr. Bradford's arm, could do to make his way over the rocks and fallen trees. Uncle Ruthven helped the ladies, and lifted the little girls over such places as were too hard for them. But Maggie would not have much help, and scrambled and climbed almost as if she had been a squirrel herself. As for Flossy, if he had made that promise of which Uncle Ruthven spoke, he certainly did not keep it.

Bessie said she thought that "wow" had meant no, not yes.

First, the mischievous puppy started a little black and white rabbit, and sent it scampering away as fast as its feet could carry it, rushing after it among all the underbrush and briars, and never heeding the coaxing calls of his little mistresses or the louder and sterner voices of their brothers; then coming back he rushed into a brook which ran by the way, and after rolling himself in it till the water was dripping from his silky coat, he shook himself and sent a shower of drops over the clean white dresses of the little girls; and then finding the hole of a woodchuck, he began scratching and burying himself in the earth in a frenzy to find the poor creature; so that, his hair being wet, he was a sight to behold when Harry pulled him out, covered with mud from head to foot, and had to be sent behind in disgrace.

The Ice Glen was truly a curious spot. A narrow pathway led through it, on one side of which was a wall of rock, so steep that not even nimble Fred could have climbed it; on the other was a shelving bank covered with tall pines and firs. It was a gloomy place where the sun never shone, and our party felt the chill from it before they entered, so that mamma said she was half afraid to have Bessie go in, so great was the change from the warm summer air without. But Mr. Bradford said there was no danger if they did not stay too long, or sit down in the glen. At the foot of the wall of rock lay great stones piled one over another; and looking through the spaces between these, the little girls saw masses of ice hard as the rock above, which lay there all the year round. How far below the surface they reached, no one knew; but there must have been a great quantity of ice there, since summer or winter, it never disappeared. Little rills and springs, cold as the ice itself, and delicious to drink, slowly trickled from each end of the glen, but though they ran all summer long, they never seemed to make any difference in the great mass which lay within. The children thought it wonderful, as indeed it was, and were very unwilling to come away when mamma said they had stayed there as long as she thought safe. They were forbidden to go there without some grown person, but this command was scarcely needed by the little girls, since Bessie could not have made her way alone without the help of some stronger hand; and though Maggie thought the glen a great curiosity, she did not like the chill and gloom of the place, and was glad to come out once more into the bright sunshine which met them at the entrance.

And here there was another thing which interested her and Bessie very much. Directly over the little stream which ran from the glen, was a small, neat, wooden building, carefully closed. The children had asked what it was when they passed it the first time, but papa said he did not know; it had been put up since he had been there last. But now they saw Fanny Porter unlocking the door, and Maggie and Bessie ran eagerly forward to ask the use of the little house.

"I'll show you," said Fanny, good-naturedly, and she threw open the door and window shutters, letting in the light and air. "This is our new dairy, Mrs. Bradford," she continued, as the older people came nearer. "Will you not walk in with the other ladies and gentlemen?"

The whole party were well pleased to enter the neat, pleasant-looking dairy. The floor was paved with large flat stones, sloping from the front and back of the building towards the middle, and through the channel thus formed was led the clear, cold stream which ran from the glen. In the icy water stood several great earthen pots, carefully covered. Around the room ran a broad shelf, also of stone, and on this were placed the bright tin pans, most of them now full of milk, and in one corner were two or three churns. The whole dairy was as neat as hands could make it, so it was quite a pleasure to think of milk and butter which should come from such a place.

"Father thought he would make the Ice Glen useful as well as curious," said Fanny Porter. "See, Mrs. Bradford, what this cold water does for our butter;" and taking the cover from one of the stone pots, she handed a wooden spaddle to the lady. Mrs. Bradford pressed it upon the butter, which she found almost as firm and hard as the rock.

"Do you make butter here?" asked Bessie.

"Indeed we do," said Fanny. "I am going to churn now, and if your mother will let you stay, you may see how I do it."

Permission was given, and the grown people went away, leaving Maggie and Bessie with the good-natured Fanny.

"Could you let us help you a little?" asked Bessie.

"Help me?" repeated Fanny, looking with a smile at the tiny figure she was just lifting upon a high stool, the only seat the dairy contained. "I guess you do not know what hard work churning is, do you?"

"Oh, we are accustomed to it," said Bessie. "We have a little churn at home, and we churn water, only it never makes butter."

"No, I suppose not," said Fanny. "And now would you like a drink after your walk?"

The children said they would, and taking down a dipper from the wall, Fanny gave them a drink of the rich, cold milk. After this she poured into the churn a quantity of thick, yellow cream, and putting on the cover, she told Bessie to stand upon the stool and go to work.

But Bessie found churning water in her own little churn at home, was a very different thing from trying to make the butter come with that heavy dasher; she could scarcely stir it, and in a moment she was quite satisfied. Maggie being stronger, pulled the dasher up and down a few times, and did not give up until she was red in the face, and her little hands were smarting with the hard work they were not used to.

The butter did not come by any means as quickly as the children expected, even when Fanny took hold; and, tired of waiting for it, they presently began to amuse themselves with sailing the acorn cups which they had picked up in their walk, in the stream which ran through the dairy. It was great fun to launch them at the upper end, and watch them as they floated down, now driven against a butter pot, now passing round it, and at last carried out at the farther end of the dairy.

By the time they had had enough of this amusement, the kind Fanny said the butter had come, and taking off the cover of the churn, she dashed in a quantity of cold water from that convenient little stream, having first lifted Maggie and Bessie upon the shelf, so that they might be high enough to look down into the churn. The butter which was floating about in tiny lumps, instantly collected together, and bringing a dish, Fanny scooped it out with a wooden ladle, and laid it in a rich, creamy mass. Then she threw in a little salt, and having worked and pressed it till it was free from every drop of water, she packed it away in a stone pot, and set that with the others in the running water. The children watched her with great interest until all was done, and were still standing by while she skimmed the cream from some of the many pans of milk, when Jane came to tell them their mamma wished them to come back to the house.

III.

A VISIT TO AUNT PATTY.

MR. BRADFORD had brought from the city a famous rockaway, or carryall, large enough to hold all his own family and one or two persons beside; light but strong, and just the thing for these mountain roads. The first use to which it was to be put was to take them all for two visits that afternoon, one to Aunt Patty, the other to the homestead where Cousin Alexander lived. It was a bright, sunny afternoon, yet not too warm to be pleasant, the air was gay with the hum of bees and butterflies, the blue sky, dappled with fleecy clouds, was reflected in the clear water, mingled with the shadow of the rocks and trees; swallows skimmed over the surface of the lake, chasing the myriads of insects which hummed in the summer air; and as the carriage drove along the road which lay between the water and the great overhanging rocks, more than one fish was seen to dart swiftly away from the shady pool where he had been snugly lying till disturbed by the rumble of the wheels.

They did not go down the mountain by the road up which they had come the night before, but struck into another which led in an opposite direction. It ran through the forest for a long distance, and was not so steep, and more shady, which was no objection on this warm day.

"Stop at Todd's cottage, if you please, Mr. Porter," said Mr. Bradford, as they came out of the forest and saw before them a small farm-house, with half a dozen out-buildings about it.

"Who is Todd, papa?" asked Maggie.

But before Mr. Bradford could answer, all curiosity about Todd, or why they were to stop at his house, was set at rest. As they turned the corner they saw, standing in the porch of the farm-house, a woman with a baby in her arms; while hanging over the gate and whistling as he looked up the road, was a boy about the size of Fred. They were Mrs. Richards and Willie, no longer "blind Willie," the sightless little child whose sad face and patient, waiting manner, had so touched the hearts of all who looked upon him. A delicate looking boy Willie was still, though two weeks' stay in this fresh, pure, mountain air had done wonders for him. It was a pretty sight to see his delight in all about him, in the sunshine and clouds, in the blue sky and the bright water, in the grass and flowers, in birds and animals, and above all in the dear faces which had been shut out from his poor eyes for so many weary months.

A light flush mounted to his pale cheeks as he caught sight of his friends in the carriage, the good, kind friends to whom he owed so much; and calling to his mother, he sprang from the gate, as Mr. Porter drew in his horses, and hastened to open it.

"Never mind, Willie," said Mr. Bradford; "we cannot come in this afternoon. Some other day, perhaps; but now we only stopped to ask how you are coming on? How do you do, Mrs. Richards?"

"Bravely, sir," answered the smiling Mrs. Richards; "and as for Willie and the baby, they are improving wonderfully, thanks to your kindness."

"It is my little girls you must thank, Mrs. Richards," said Mr. Bradford.

"But we don't want to be thanked," said Bessie, quickly. "We quite liked to have you come up here, Mrs. Richards, and we felt very much thankful ourselves when Uncle Ruthven gave us the money to send you."

"Willie," said Maggie, "do you enjoy being *disblinded* just as much as you did at first?"

"Oh, yes," answered Willie, laughing at Maggie's new word; "and everything looks so much nicer than it did before I was blind. Somehow, I think the world *did* grow prettier while I could not see it, though mother says it only seems so to me."

"Ah, that is often the way, Willie," said Mr. Bradford. "God sometimes has to teach us the worth of the blessings He has given us by taking them from us."

After a little more talk with Willie and his mother, they bade good-by; kind Mr. Porter first saying he would send down for Willie some day and let him come up to his place.

They drove on till they came to the more open country, and saw before them Aunt Patty's house, and beyond that, the grand old homestead of which they had heard so much, and of which papa was so fond.

Aunt Patty's home was a pretty, snug cottage on the side of a hill; its front covered with a beautiful trumpet creeper, which went climbing up to the very top of the many-cornered old chimney, and wreathing itself over the little porch and the bow window of the sitting-room, until the house looked like a quiet green nest. A great white cat peeped out from behind the geraniums which filled the window; a greyhound lay upon the doormat, and beneath and about the porch hung several bird-cages, containing half a dozen canaries and two mocking-birds, while a donkey and a tame goat looked, the one over, the other between the bars of the fence which divided their little pasture ground from the neat garden. For Aunt Patty was very fond of dumb pets, and had collected about her a number, each one of which knew her voice, and would come at her call; and she was never sharp and short with them as she sometimes was with her own fellow creatures, for they never, even by accident, gave her offence.

The old lady herself came to the door to meet her guests, more pleased than she would have been willing to say, that they had come to visit her on the first day of their stay at Chalecoo. She seized Frankie in her arms and covered him with kisses; but that roguish young gentleman after exclaiming, "Hallo, Patty!" would have nothing more to say to her, and struggled to be set free that he might run and see "dat nanny-doat and dat pony wis long ears."

Maggie and Bessie were more polite than their little brother, and though they would have liked to follow him at once, waited quietly till Aunt Patty asked them if they did not wish to run about and make acquaintance with all her pets.

Glad of the permission, the little girls ran out, and turned to the paddock, where they found Frankie seated upon the donkey's back.

The boys had not gone into the house, but after shaking hands with Aunt Patty at the door, had remained without in search of what amusement they could find. The donkey was the first thing that had taken their attention as well as that of Frankie; and when the little fellow came out clamoring for a ride, they were quite ready to indulge him. Harry had been half doubtful if they had not better first ask Aunt Patty's permission, but Fred had said,—

"Pooh! what's the use? She would let Frankie dance on her own head, if he wanted to."

So Harry had allowed himself to be persuaded, and in another moment the donkey, much to his own astonishment, found Frankie seated upon his back.

Now this donkey was not at all accustomed to children; for those of Mr. Alexander Bradford, who lived at the homestead, seldom came to see Aunt Patty, and when they did so, they would as soon have thought of asking to ride upon her back as upon that of the donkey. To be harnessed in the little pony-carriage, and trot about with the old lady for her daily drive, was all the work to which Nonesuch was used; and when he found Frankie perched upon him, he was very much displeased, and began a series of antics and prancings which were more becoming some frisky pony than a sober, well-behaved donkey. But try as he would, he could not shake Frankie off. The bold little rogue was not at all frightened, and clung like a burr to his indignant steed. It was hard to tell which would come off victor. But at the side of the paddock ran one of the many streams in which this mountain country rejoiced, shadowed with a growth of elder, sumach, and other high bushes. Nonesuch had raced with Frankie to the very edge of this little rivulet, and then stood still for a moment as if considering what he would do next, when a hand, holding a long, thorny switch, was suddenly put forth from the clump of bushes, and Nonesuch received a stinging blow across his haunches. Down went the donkey's nose and up went his heels, as he sent Frankie flying directly over his head into the stream, and then tore away to the further side of the field.

Maggie and Bessie were very much startled, and screamed aloud, and even Harry and Fred were a good deal alarmed; but the child himself did not seem to be at all frightened, and when his brothers pulled him out of the water, did not cry, but looked after the donkey in great surprise, exclaiming, —

"Why, dat pony spilled me a little!"

Harry and Fred laughed at this, but Maggie and Bessie thought it no laughing matter; nor did mamma, when alarmed by their screams the grown people came running from the house. Frankie was drenched from head to foot, and had to be carried at once to the house, undressed and rubbed dry. Then he was wrapped in a blanket, while a messenger was sent to the homestead to borrow some clothes for him. The little fellow thought this rather hard, and a very poor ending to his afternoon's amusement, especially when no clothes could be found to fit him but those of little Katy Bradford.

Meanwhile Fred was off, no one knew where. At the moment Frankie had gone over the donkey's head a loud mocking laugh had resounded from behind the clump of bushes, as though the person who had given the blow were rejoicing in the mischief he had done.

Fred only waited to see Frankie safely out of the water, and then, leaving him to the care of his brother and sisters, darted across the stream and forced his way through the bushes in search of the guilty person. At a little distance from him stood two miserable looking objects, a boy about his own size, a girl rather younger; both dirty, ragged, and half-starved, hatless and shoeless. A wicked looking boy and girl they were too, and as Fred appeared they greeted him with grimaces and vulgar noises; then as he darted at the boy, turned and ran.

Fred gave chase, and in a moment had overtaken the girl. But hot-tempered and hasty though he was, Fred was not the boy to fight with one who was weaker than himself; and he passed her without notice, keeping on after her companion. But active as he was, he soon found he was no match for the young rascal in front of him, whose feet scarcely seemed to touch the ground, and who threw himself headlong over fences and hedges, as though he had forgotten he had a neck and limbs which might be broken.

So turning about, Fred went after the girl, and soon had his hand upon her arm, calling upon her to stop. She did so, at the same time cowering and raising the other arm to shield her head and face as if expecting a blow.

"You don't think I am going to strike you?" said Fred, "a nice kind of a chap I'd be to strike a girl. I say, what did you hit that donkey for?"

"I didn't," she replied sullenly, "it was him."

"What did he do it for? Nobody was doing anything to him. And I'll be bound you had the will to do it."

"He did it cos he had a mind to," she said, shaking herself free from Fred's hold, "and he'll do it agin if he has a mind to."

"He'd better not," said Fred, "if he does, I'll fix him."

" S'posin' you can catch him," she answered, growing bold and impudent, as she saw she need fear no violence from Fred. " Taint none of your donkeys."

" It was my little brother he meant to plague though," said Fred. " He'd better look out how he troubles us again. Just you tell him that."

" He aint afraid of you," said the girl, " I jist hope the young un's fine clothes was spoiled. Good enough for him," and making up a hideous face at Fred she ran off a few steps, and then as if the spirit of mischief within her were too strong even for her fear of him, stooped, and picking up a large stone threw it with all her strength. It hit Fred upon the knee with such force that, brave as he was, he could scarcely help crying aloud, and was obliged to sit down upon the ground until the pain had somewhat passed. By the time he was on his feet again the girl was out of sight, and poor Fred limped back to Aunt Patty's cottage.

Here the bruised and swollen knee was bathed and bound up, but Fred was forced to keep still, not only this afternoon, but for several succeeding days.

It would be hard to tell with what horror the children looked upon the boy and girl whom Fred described, and who had done all this unprovoked mischief.

After the donkey and goat, the birds, kittens and other pets had been visited, there was not much to interest the children in Aunt Patty's house; and they were not very sorry when the visit came to an end, and they were all on their way to the homestead.

There was certainly enough to please them here. It was a grand old house, standing in the midst of a grove of maples, and behind it stretched an immense orchard, with its mossy old apple trees giving promise of the rich harvest they would furnish a few months later. There was the flower garden, delicious with all kinds of roses now in full bloom; the very swing where papa used to swing when he was a boy, the stream and pond where he used to sail his boats and set up his water-mills; and beyond all, the large farm-yard with its many outbuildings, looking almost like a village by itself; while from one of the great barns whose wide doors stood open came the cackling of poultry and cooing of pigeons, the lowing of cows and oxen, and bleating of calves, all the pleasant noises of a large and thrifty farm.

The children were all anxious to see the spot where the old burnt barn had stood, the place where Aunt Patty had saved Uncle Aleck from the fire; but all trace both of fire and barn had long since passed away, and a bright green pasture field, where a flock of sheep were feeding, took up the very ground where, as Maggie said, " the story had happened."

The children of the homestead, eight in number, of all ages and sizes, from cousin Ernest, a tall youth of eighteen, down to little

Katy, the household darling and pet of four, were only too glad to welcome their city cousins and show them all the wonders of the place.

They had the most delightful summer playroom; one side of the verandah enclosed with a lattice work, covered with flowering vines, where they kept their bats and balls, graces, hoops, rocking horse and other toys. They had a little garden house too, where they kept their spades, rakes and other tools, for each child had a plot of ground for its own, and every fall they had a flower and fruit show, when their father and mother gave prizes, not only for the best flowers and fruit, but also to those whose gardens had been neatly kept during the summer.

Poor Fred with his lame knee could not run about with the others, and as he sat on the verandah with his cousin Ernest, who stayed with him lest he should be lonely, and heard all about the flower show, he began to wish that he and his brother could have something of the same kind.

"I dare say Mr. Porter would give us each a little piece of ground," he said, "but then it is too late to plant things, is it not?"

"Oh, no," replied his cousin, "it is only the middle of June, and there are several things which you might yet plant. Then you could join us and try for the prizes at our show, and I would ask father to have it a little earlier in the fall, before you go home. There are lots of seeds and plants that we will give you if you have a mind to try."

Fred was eager enough, as he always was for every thing new, and promised to ask his brother if he would like to have a garden, and also to speak to his father and Mr. Porter about it.

"And your sisters, too," said Ernest, "would they not like to try what they could do?"

"Oh! they are too little," said Fred. "What could such a mite as Bessie do with a garden of her own? She might dig and plant in it to be sure, but then she would not know how to take care of her flowers and things, and she would only be disappointed if she failed."

"You and Harry might help her," said Ernest, "and even if she did not have any fine flowers she might gain a prize if she had been industrious, and tried as well as she knew how. It is not so much for the worth and beauty of the flowers themselves, as for the pains we have taken with them and what we deserve, that father rewards us. Why, last year dear little Katy took a prize and for what do you think? Why, for a poor forlorn zinnia which she had nursed through the whole summer, and which bore but one scanty flower."

"I'll tell Maggie and Bessie then," said Fred, "and Harry and I will do all we can to help them with the work that is too hard for them. I am sure papa will be willing for us to try, if your father will allow us to join you."

"He is willing enough," said Ernest, "indeed he was saying the other day he should like it. You had better ask Mr. Porter for the ground and begin directly."

Fred was so anxious to talk over this new plan with his brother and sisters, and to ask his father and Mr. Porter what they thought of it, that he could scarcely wait to do so till it was time to go home.

IV.

LEM AND DOLLY.

As soon as they were all once more in the carriage, and the horses' heads turned homeward, Fred told what Ernest had proposed. Mr. Bradford willingly gave permission for his children to join their cousins in preparing for the flower show, and promised to furnish whatever seeds and plants it would be best for them to have, in case Mr. Porter could give them the ground.

"That I will," said the old man readily. "And, by the way, there's a plot in the lower part of the garden that will be just about the right thing for you. There's nothing planted there yet, for I only took it in this spring, but it has been all dug and raked over, and is ready for whatever is to go in it. I'll give you boys each ten feet square, and the girls six. I guess that's about as much as they can manage."

"More, I fear," said Mrs. Bradford, "at least such little hands as those of my Bessie, are scarcely strong enough for work that could raise any flowers fit to take a prize."

"But we will help her, mamma," said Fred "and if she tries, and cousin Alexander thinks she has done her best, that is all that is necessary." And he told the story of little Katy and her zinnia.

"I may try, mamma, may I not?" said Bessie earnestly, "Katy is a very little girl, only four years old; and I am quite old, you know, for I was six last month."

"Certainly you may try, my very old girl," said mamma, kissing the little, eager, upturned face; "and I will do all I can to help you; but then if you and Maggie do not take the prizes you must not be too much disappointed."

"Oh! no, and I can have satis — fac — tion

in my garden any way, mamma," said Bessie, "in 'tending to it and watering it; and then I can give my flowers to you and Aunt May and every one else I love, and that will be enough of pleasure for me."

Mamma smiled and thanked her, and thought if her dear little girl were to give flowers to every one who loved *her* she would need a very large garden with a great many blossoms in it.

Mr. Porter knew that Frankie had been in the water, but he had not heard how the accident came about, nor of its after consequences; and now, as he saw Fred moving restlessly to ease his aching knee, he asked him how he had been hurt.

Fred told the story of Frankie's ducking, of his own chase after the mischief-makers, and of what had happened to himself.

"Whew — ew — ew!" said Mr. Porter, as he finished, "I am sorry to hear this; sorry enough, sorry enough. Can you tell me what kind of looking boy and girl they were?"

Fred described the boy and girl, as nearly as he could, and Mr. Porter gave another long dismayed whistle.

"Yes, I thought so," he said, "there's no one here about but those two who would have been up to such an ugly trick as that. So, they're back again. I hoped we were rid of them for good and all."

"Who are they?" asked Mr. Bradford.

"Lem and Dolly Owen, sir; as bad a pair, and the children of as bad a father as one could find on a long summer day. Poor neglected creatures, they are to be pitied too; but it is useless to try to do anything for them, for all help is worse than thrown away. They live in a little tumble-down shanty back of the rocks at the lower end of the lake, and a terrible nuisance they are to me and every one in the neighborhood. The father is a drunkard of the worst sort, the mother long since dead, and these two children, liars, vagabonds and thieves, up to every sort of wicked mischief, and a terror to all the children in

Chalecoo. They live as they can, by robbing orchards, hen-roosts, dairies and corn-fields during the summer; picking up odd bits, and stealing whatever they can lay their fingers on in the winter, half starved and half frozen the most of the time."

"Can nothing be done for them?" asked Mr. Bradford.

"No, sir; as I say, it is not worth while to try to help them. All that the father can lay his hands on he spends in drink. My wife was distressed about the children, especially the girl, to think she should be growing up in such wickedness and misery; and last winter she fixed up a suit of warm clothes for her, and coaxing her into the house with a deal of trouble, for she is as wild as a hawk, she dressed her in them, and promised to give her and her brother a good meal every day if they would come quietly to the house and get it. My dear old woman hoped she might do them both some good if she could but keep a hold on them in this way. But the girl just took what she could get that day as sullenly as you please, never speaking a word of thanks, and making no promises, though she did look mighty proud of her new clothes, and hugged herself up in them as if she were glad to feel herself in something warm and comfortable. My wife, knowing what a thief she was, watched her all the time, and thought she could not possibly carry off anything; but somehow the sly creature got the better of her, and she had scarcely gone when a china plate was missed. Now my wife set a deal by that plate, for it had been hers when she was a little child, and the boys set out at once in search of Dolly. Well, will you believe it? no sooner did she catch sight of them, and guess what they were after, than she just dashed the plate down on the rocks, smashing it to atoms, and ran like a deer. They'd promised their mother not to hurt her, so they let her go; but the next day she was seen in all her old rags, and we found the new clothes had been sold by Owen at the next village. Of course they went for liquor, and that's the way everything goes. Kindness is all wasted on the children; they'll take what you give them with one hand, and steal from you with the other, and then abuse you for what you've done for them."

"Did Dolly and her brother come to get the nice meal kind Mrs. Porter promised them?" asked Bessie.

"No, indeed; they've kept clear enough of the family ever since; not that they are ashamed, but afraid."

"I should think they ought to be ashamed," said Maggie, indignantly. "I never heard of such ungratefulness, and Mrs. Porter ought to serve Dolly right, and never do another thing for her; she don't deserve it."

"Ah! my little girl, if we were all served right, and had nothing but what we deserve, where would we be?" said the old man. "But that did just discourage my wife, and she has left the wretched creatures to themselves since. She saw it was of no use. Owen won't leave his children a decent thing to their backs, a bed to sleep on, or a cup or plate to eat from. My old woman is not the first that has taken pity on them, and tried to make them a little comfortable; but whatever is given them just goes for drink, drink; and we have all given it up as a hopeless job. Besides, the children themselves are so lawless and thankless, that every kindness that is done for them they only turn into a means of mischief."

"Does the father ill-treat them?" asked Mrs. Bradford.

"Yes, he not only encourages them to steal and lie, but beats them when they bring nothing home which he can exchange for liquor. We often hear their cries away up at my house, but there's no way of stopping it, as I see."

"And must these poor children just be left to go to ruin?" asked Mrs. Bradford, sadly.

"There's no one can reach them to teach them better, I am afraid," said Mr. Porter.

"You'll just get hard words and worse for your pains if you try it. Why, there was the clergyman from down in the village, came up to see them, and he brought along a bundle of good things and gave them to Dolly; and while he was talking kindly to her, he got a blow on the back with a big stone, and others came about him thick and fast. He knew it was Lem, but what could he do? He could not see the boy or fix it on him. And that's the way; they are both so sly and artful, they are seldom or never caught in the act; so though when a melon patch or hen-roost is robbed, or some fine young trees are hacked to pieces, every one feels sure it was Lem or Dolly who did the mischief, yet it is difficult to prove it on them. Lem has had more thrashings than any boy of his size that ever lived, I believe, but what's the use? It only makes him worse than ever. Farmer Grafton caught him once stealing clothes from the bleaching-ground, and handed him over to the constable for a few days; but that night his hay-ricks were burnt down. Folks first thought it was Owen that did it, but he was proved to have lain dead drunk all night in the liquor shop down in the village; and then everybody believed it was Doll, and with reason too, for she's just bad enough to do it, young as she is. Last March they all went off, father and children, and I did hope we should see no more of them; but here the young ones are back, it seems. I trust Owen is not with them. If you little ones come to me to-night, I'll tell you what old Sol here did for that fellow, and how the dumb beast showed himself the wisest of the two."

"I am very sorry for Lem and Dolly," said Bessie. "If their mother had not died maybe they would not have been so naughty. It's very sorrowful for children not to have any mamma to teach them better. Don't they have any one to love them, Mr. Porter?"

"Well, they seem to love one another after their own rude fashion," answered Mr. Porter.

"It's about the only mark of good that's left in them."

"I wish we could do something to make them a little better," said Bessie.

"The Lord love you for the wish," said Mr. Porter, looking kindly around at her, "but you could never do anything, you little lamb. Why, they'd tease you out of your senses if you went to speak to them, and they're not fit for the like of you to notice either. Just you keep out of their way as much as you can, dearie, or they'll do you a mischief if they find the chance."

Mr. Bradford here began to talk of something else, and they all forgot Lem and Dolly for the time. But as they were about half way home, Fred, who was sitting in front with Mr. Porter, suddenly exclaimed,—

"There are those children!" and looking before them, they all saw the ragged, miserable boy and girl standing on a stone at a little distance from the road side.

As the carriage approached, they darted

away into the woods, but soon after a shower of gravel and sand flying into the carriage, as it slowly toiled up a hill between two walls of rock, made it known in a very disagreeable manner that they had returned to annoy our party by further mischief. They kept out of sight behind the trees and rocks, however; and when Fred, who was furiously angry, begged Mr. Porter to go after them with his long whip, the loud, taunting laugh which rang from above told that their tormentors felt themselves secure from punishment.

The carriage was soon beyond this narrow pass, and they saw and heard no more of Lem and Dolly, and reached home without further mischief.

"Why, how long you stayed," said good Mrs. Porter, coming out as they drove up to the door. "I waited to feed the chickens, as I promised the dear little girls here; but I am afraid they want their supper badly. Come along, my darlings," and with a pan in each hand, and followed by Maggie, Bessie and Frankie, the kind old lady went out to feed the fowls.

"Margaret and Bessie, come here," said Mr. Stanton, calling his wife and sister to the door as they passed through the hall. "Is not that a picture?"

A picture it was indeed, and one which mamma thought so pretty that she had to call the rest of the family to enjoy it. Beneath a great spreading pear-tree sat the motherly old lady, the last golden rays of the setting sun falling over her ample figure, in her neat black gown, white apron, and snowy kerchief folded over her bosom, spectacles in hand, and in her lap the pan which held the corn and barley; while around her were the three little ones dipping their chubby hands into the measure, and scattering the contents among the noisy, scrambling crowd of fowls, themselves full of glee and happiness at this, to them, new pleasure.

There was one jealous old fellow, a pet rooster and a great beauty, who would take

Bessie among the Mountains. p. 81.

his supper from no hand but that of his mistress; and flying on the bench beside her, he courted her notice and a supper by himself. Mrs. Porter was about to indulge him, but Flossy, who was seated by her, watching with great satisfaction the feeding of the chickens, seemed to think it quite unfair that he should not take his chance with the others, and soon chased him from the bench. Upon which the rooster refused to eat at all, and after pecking one or two of the smaller chickens pretty severely, he strutted away with his neck stretched very straight, and expressing his displeasure in a loud and by no means pleasant voice. In vain did Mrs. Porter call him by his name, "Coxcomb," which he knew quite well; he only flapped his wings and walked farther away, screaming louder than ever.

"He is a very naughty bird, and now he must just go without any supper," said Maggie.

"Ah! my poor Coxcomb," said Mrs. Porter, "don't you think he is pretty?"

"Yes," said Maggie, "he is very pretty but

he is not a bit good. He is not at all 'handsome is that handsome does—' pecking that dear little yellow chicken! I'd rather be that brown guinea hen who is so nice and good, even if she is not so very pretty."

"Yes, yes," said Mrs. Porter, "that is the way, all the beauty in the world will not make us loved if we are not kind and sweet."

The feeding of the fowls was scarcely done when they were called in to their own supper; and when this was over, our little girls with their elder brothers ran off to find Mr. Porter, and beg for the story about old Sol.

The old man was seated outside the kitchen door, enjoying the lovely summer twilight, and waiting, he said, to see if the children would not come to claim his promise. He took Bessie upon his knee, and bade Fanny bring a stool for Maggie, while Harry and poor limping Fred, who came slowly after the others, sat upon the curb stone which ran around the old well.

"It was just about this time last year," began Mr. Porter, when they were all settled, "that I hired a new farm hand. His name was Ted, and he was a simple, half witted fellow, easily led by those about him. I don't think he had much judgment or conscience of his own, poor lad, but was ready to do either right or wrong according as he was persuaded at the moment. Tell him to do a certain thing in a certain way and he would obey, unless some one else came along and told him differently; when he would do as the last speaker said, and forget all his former orders. He meant to be faithful, but of course he was not to be trusted without a good deal of watching to make sure he was not interfered with, and there were folks enough, bad boys and girls, who were always ready to meddle with him and set him up to some mischief, just for the bit of fun it would make for themselves. He was the son of a poor widow in the village, who had hard work to keep herself and her seven children fed and warmed through the winter; and Ted, who was ready enough to help his mother so far as he knew how, could get no steady work. No one had patience with the simple lad who was so easily led astray without intending to do wrong; and who would come and confess his mistakes with the most triumphant air, believing that he must have done right since he had obeyed the last orders he had received.

"But I thought with me and the boys to look after him, he could get along here, so I hired him. He was a capital hand with horses, and his work was mostly about the stable, feeding the horses, rubbing them down and the like. He used to pet the dumb creatures and talk to them as if they were human beings, and it was wonderful to see how fond they all became of him, old Sol in particular. He would run to meet Ted, and follow him about the fields just as your little Flossy there follows you; or if he was in the stable would whinny with delight the moment he heard his step.

"Ted had a way of curling himself up in

Sol's manger and going to sleep when his work was done, and the horse would never suffer any one to come near or disturb him till he had had his nap out.

"Well, so Ted was doing very well, being obedient and industrious, when one day about Christmas time my son Bill went down to the steamboat landing to bring up a load of stores which had been brought from the city. There was a deep snow on the ground, with a prospect of more to come that day, and I did not feel just so willing to have him caught in the storm. A snow storm on these mountain roads is not a nice thing to be out in, I can tell you; but some of the stores were pretty badly wanted, and we were afraid they would spoil, lying on the dock.

"So Bill started off, taking Ted with him to help him load up, and driving Sol and Nero before the sledge.

"When he reached the village he went to the post-office, where he found a letter to himself, telling him his favorite brother Walter, who was at college in the city, was very ill and wanted to see him. There was but an hour or two before the train would be along, not time enough for him to come up home and go back again; so he went to the dock, loaded up the sledge, and giving the reins to Ted, bade him go straight home and stop for nothing.

"Ted would have done this had he been let alone; but as he came back through the village, a lot of mischievous fellows got hold of him and told him he was to stop at the public house and rest his horses before they set out for their pull up the mountain. When they had persuaded him they led him on to drink, till he became noisy and more foolish than ever; and when they had had their fun with him they let him go.

"As he was leaving, Seth Owen came out with his jug of whiskey and begged to be taken up the mountain. Now I had many times warned Ted against Owen, for I knew he was just the one to lead the poor fellow wrong if it was only to spite me; but he told Ted I had sent orders he was to take him home, and the lad was persuaded to do it.

"I suppose after they were on their way, Owen drank afresh himself, and led Ted to do the same. However that was, the hours went by, and when Bill did not come I began to be uneasy, all the more as by this time it was snowing heavily. I was standing on the piazza, looking down the road, and thinking if it was not best to yoke up a team of oxen and go in search of my boy, when I saw the sledge coming up the side of the lake. But no Bill and no Ted were with it, the horses were alone, plodding along through the snow, and if ever it was said without words, 'there's something wrong, come as quick as you can,' old Sol said it that day. We pitched off the load, quick as lightning, and I, with my other boys, started in search of Ted. My fears for Bill were set at rest by finding, pinned to one of the bags, a note saying where he had gone; for the dear thoughtful fellow had been afraid Ted would forgot to give it to me, and so put it where he knew I must see it.

"Sol and Nero went straight ahead without orders or guidance, for I just let them have the rein, thinking the faithful creatures knew better than I did where they should go. Half way down the mountain they went, and night was just beginning to fall, when they stopped short in one of the most break-neck places on the whole road. We looked about us, and there, sticking up out of the snow, was a man's leg. We pulled him out in less than no time, but it was not poor Ted, but Seth Owen. We searched all about for the poor lad in vain; when, seeing old Sol was mighty uneasy, and stretching his neck out as if he wanted to get free, I took him out of the harness, thinking the creature might help us.

"Sure enough, he turned about, and going to a spot where the mountain fell sheer down a hundred feet or so, he pawed away the snow, and there, half on, half over the edge of the precipice, hung Ted, his clothes caught by a bush, and holding him back from sure destruction. He, as well as Owen, was dead drunk.

"We were putting him on the sledge when I saw Sol, who had trotted back to the place where we found Owen, pawing away once more at the snow, snorting and sniffing as if he were displeased. I went to see what he was about, thinking here was some other fellow buried in the snow; but as I came up to him, he uncovered the whiskey jug, the cause of all this mischief. He smelled about it for a moment, and then, with a snort of disgust, turned about, and dashing his heels upon it, sent it flying over the cliff, then walked quietly to the sledge, and placed himself ready to be harnessed, with an air which said, 'That can do no more harm.' We lost no time in getting home, where Ted, and Owen too, were brought round with difficulty. An hour more and they would both have been frozen to death. So you may believe we have cause to think much of old Sol."

"But how did the two men happen to fall from the sledge so nearly in the same place?" said Harry.

"We supposed they were both stupefied, partly by drink, partly with the cold, and that the sledge had run upon the bank, causing it to tip sideways, and they had slipped off, while the load being securely fastened with ropes had remained in its place."

"And did Ted ever get drunk again?" Bessie.

"Not while he was with me," said Mr. Porter, "and I hope he never will again. When he was told of his narrow escape and of what old Sol had done, he said, 'Nice old horse, nice old horse, he knew better than Ted. He teach Ted never touch whiskey stuff again.' His mother moved out west this spring, and he went with her; but I think his poor dull brain has received a lesson it will never forget."

"And what did Owen say about his jug?" asked Fred.

"He was very angry, and swore he would make me pay for it, seeming to think little of the saving of his life since he had lost that. He managed to pick up another one in a day or two, and the lesson did him no good."

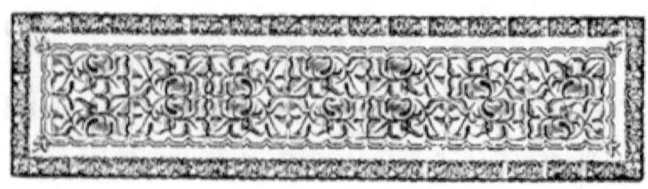

V.

THE GARDENS.

BESSIE thought a great deal of those two poor, wicked, neglected children, who had no one to care for them; and when she went up to bed and had knelt at her mother's side, and said her evening prayers, she paused a moment before she rose and said, —

"Please, dear Jesus, send some one to teach Lem and Dolly about you, and how you loved little children, and let me help them a little if there is any way I could do it, 'cause I am so sorry for them. Amen."

Mamma laid her hand very tenderly on her darling's head, though she said nothing, for she did not see how it was possible for her gentle little girl to help the two forlorn outcasts upon whom all kindness seemed worse than thrown away.

"Yet who knows what even she might do?" thought the mother, as having seen each little birdling safe in its nest, she went slowly and musingly down stairs to join the rest of the family, thinking as she went of Bessie's simple prayer, "who knows what even she might do? for —

> 'Often such *childish* heart is brought
> To act with power beyond its thought,
> For God by ways they have not known
> Will lead his own.'"

It would not be the first time, as the mother knew, that the seed innocently dropped by that baby hand had taken root, and brought forth fruit rich and flourishing in the garden of the Lord.

"Maggie," said Bessie, the next morning as they sat together upon the piazza step, waiting for Mr. Porter to take them to the garden and give them their plots of ground, "Maggie, would you not like to do something for Lem and Dolly?"

"Yes, that I would," said Maggie; "I would just like to give Lem a good soaking in the lake, and to make Dolly's knee hurt just as much as Fred's."

"But that would be naughty," said Bessie; "it's not the way Jesus would like us to do, and it's not the Golden Rule that you like so much, Maggie. I think it is to give evil for evil."

"Well, I s'pose it is," said Maggie; "and it is rather naughty, I do believe, Bessie; but I do not mean I would do it, only I would like to do it. I think I'll be about as naughty as that."

"Don't you think you can forgive them, Maggie?"

"No, not quite," said Maggie. "I'll forgive them a little, but I can't give them the whole of my forgiveness. Why, they were so very bad, and did so many mean things to us, when we did not do a single thing to them.

Don't you feel a bit angry with them, Bessie?"

"Yes," said Bessie, "I'm 'fraid I do. When I think about it I feel pretty angry. But I want to try and forgive them enough to do a kind thing to them if I have a chance."

"Oh," said Maggie, "we could never do a kind thing to them even if we wanted to. You see they just come and do something bad, and then run away, 'cause their guilty conscience knows they ought to be punished. And besides, Bessie, they're not fit 'ciety for us. The copy book says, 'Shun evil company,' and mamma said that meant we must not go with wicked people. And they are so ragged and dirty. You would not like to touch them or sit down by them, would you?"

"No," said Bessie, quickly, for she was very dainty and delicate in all her ways, and the thought of coming near the miserable, dirty children was not at all pleasant to her; " but maybe sometimes we might say a kind word to them without going very close to them; and if we showed them we did not feel very mad with them, perhaps they would not be so naughty to us. I am so very sorry for them, 'cause they have no one to teach them better, and no mother, and such a bad father, who tries to make them more wicked. If you ever had the chance to do a little bit of kindness for them, Maggie, would you not do it?"

"I don't know," said Maggie, "that's a great thing to make up my resolution about, and I'll have to think about it a little. Oh, here are Mr. Porter and the boys. Now let us go."

"Maggie and Bessie, mamma wants to speak to you in her room before you go," said Harry, looking very full of glee.

The little girls ran in, and there, oh, delight! there stood mamma with a tiny spade, rake and hoe in each hand. It was quite impossible to mistake who they were meant for. They were just of the right size for our two small gardeners; and mamma's look and smile as she held them out told that they were for their use.

Maggie gave a shriek of delight and went capering all about the room; and Bessie's bright smile and the color which flushed her cheeks told that though less noisy, she was not less pleased than her sister.

"Oh, you darling, precious mamma," said Maggie, pausing in her capers to examine the pretty toys, "they are just what we wanted. How did you get them so quickly?"

"I brought them with me," said mamma, "thinking that some day when you wanted something to do, they might furnish you with a new pleasure; but I did not think they would prove useful so soon. You must be careful of them, and not leave them lying out in the damp, or they will be spoiled."

The children readily promised, and ran off to show their treasures to their brothers and Mr. Porter.

Mr. Porter soon measured off such a square of ground as he had promised for each of them, adding one for Hafed, who was much pleased to do as the others, and fell to with a good will at digging and planting. Mr. Porter also kindly gave them such seeds as would do to plant at this late season; and papa, who had driven down to the village with the Colonel and Uncle Ruthven, came back with a number of verbenas, heliotropes, geranium slips and other pretty things, which were set out in the new gardens. Nor was this all, for Uncle Ruthven had bought a small watering-pot for each child, and they had gone to the carpenter's, where the Colonel had ordered two wheel-barrows, one of a fit size for Maggie and Bessie, the other a little larger for the boys, and these were to be done in a day or two. In short, nothing seemed wanting to success but patience and industry on the part of the young gardeners.

The girls chose to have only flowers in their gardens, but the boys had some vegetables as well. Mr. Porter told them the beds must be kept nicely weeded, and watered when the weather was dry.

There was only one fault which Maggie and Bessie could find with their gardens, and that was that they lay at such a distance from the house that mamma could not allow them to go there without their brothers or nurse to have an eye upon them. Not that they were not to be trusted out of sight, but mamma did not think it safe for two such little girls.

For some days after this, the four boys, Harry, Fred, Hafed and Bob, seemed to have an immense amount of whittling to do. At all odd times they were found with their knives and small strips of wood in their hands, and these bits of wood were all fashioned into one size and shape. But to what use they were to be put was kept a grand secret, until one day when Maggie and Bessie went with Jane to work in their gardens, they found a neat little fence about five inches high all around their plots. The kind brothers had made this agreeable little surprise for them.

"Our peoples are always doing nice things for us," said Bessie, when they had thanked the boys.

"Yes," said Maggie, "I am quite expecting to be surprised all the time."

At which the Colonel and Mrs. Rush, who were standing by, laughed, though Maggie could not see why.

Meanwhile nothing more had been seen or heard of Lem and Dolly. Mr. Porter had found out that Owen had not returned with them, and that the two children were alone in their miserable shanty. One day when Maggie and Bessie were out walking with some of their older friends, they came upon this wretched home, if home it could be called. The rock against which it leaned formed one side of the house, the other three were of single boards nailed together. A square hole was cut for a window, but had neither glass nor casement; and the door hung by one rusty hinge, which looked as if it might give way at any moment. There was no one about; Lem and Dolly were away, probably busied in some new mischief or theft, and our party peeped within the open door. No furniture of any kind was there. A heap of dried leaves and dirty rags upon the hard, uneven ground which formed the floor, was the only bed; and the little girls drew back in disgust. Without, upon the rocks, were the charred embers of a fire, and over them two crooked sticks, and they, with a battered tin pan, and numberless bones and feathers which lay scattered about, told that there the ill-gotten food was cooked and eaten.

It must have been a hard heart which was not saddened by the thought that this was all the home of two young children; and Bessie felt more pity than ever for Lem and Dolly. Maggie felt it, too, and as they turned away, she whispered to her sister, —

"Bessie, I never saw such a dreadful place to live in. I *would* do a kind thing for Lem and Dolly, if I could."

It was a lovely spot, too, but for the signs of

poverty and filth around. Before them the mountain fell suddenly away, leaving on two sides a beautiful view of the open country, dotted with its fields and farm-houses. Away to the north stretched range after range of blue hills, till those in the distance were lost in the veil of mist which hung over their tops. The woods around were full of wild flowers, briar roses, delicate primroses, and the bright red columbine, and even here and there, a late anemone; the little star-like flower, looking almost as if it had dropped from heaven, and wondered to find itself alone and solitary, so far away from its sister stars.

A perfect silence lay upon all around; not a sound was heard; not a leaf seemed to stir in the summer air; not a bird was heard to utter a note; and a hush fell upon the party as they turned into the lovely little woodpath which led them homeward.

Bessie lingered a little, with her eyes fixed far away, and her head on one side as if she were hearkening to something.

"What is it, darling?" asked her father. "Are you not ready to go?"

"Yes, papa," she answered, putting her hand into his; "I was only listening to the still."

Her father smiled, and led her on till they had joined the rest. They were quite near home when the Colonel, who had fallen a little behind with his wife, called to Maggie and Bessie.

"To-morrow is Sunday," he said. "Have you found a place where you can have your Sunday-school class?"

No, Maggie and Bessie said, they had not thought of it.

"But perhaps Mr. Porter will let us have it in one of his barns, as Mr. Jones used to do last summer," said Bessie.

"I have found a better place than that for you," said Colonel Rush; "that is, on a pleasant Sunday. When it rains, we must find cover within doors. See, here, what do you think of this for a Sunday-school room?"

And he guided them a little to one side, where a sloping path and four or five natural steps led down into a broad crevice or cleft among the rocks which surrounded the lake.

A lovely room it was indeed, carpeted with moss, curtained and shaded by the green trees which waved overhead, and furnished with seats made by one or two fallen stones on one side, on the other by a ledge of rock which jutted out at just such a height as to make a convenient bench for little people. The steps by which they had descended, closed them in behind; in front lay the lake; beyond that again the gray old rocks, the mountain rising bold and stern above the peaceful waters. No glimpse of the Lake House or its cheerful surroundings could be seen, unless one peered around the edge of the inclosing mass of rock, and this the Colonel would not permit the children to do, lest they should fall into the water which washed at the very foot of the pretty retreat.

The little ones were enchanted, as was their

dear teacher, Mrs Rush, or "Aunt May," as they always called her now.

"I thought you would like it," said the Colonel. "I was strolling about this morning when I came upon this nook, and thought what a pleasant Sunday-school room it would make. So convenient, too. See, this great stone will do for a seat for May, and here is one for her table; while this ledge makes a capital resting-place for you. Try it, little ones."

The bench certainly did very well for Maggie, but Bessie's feet would not touch the ground. However, the Colonel made that all right by rolling over a flat stone which answered for a footstool, and Maggie and Bessie thought there was nothing more to be desired.

"Harry and Fred want to come," said Bessie, "do you think you could let them, Aunt May? Sunday evening we always tell them the stories the Colonel tells us in the morning, but they say they would like to hear them for themselves."

"And Uncle Ruthven would like Hafed to come too," said Maggie. "He said he was going to ask you. Hafed likes to learn, Aunt May, and he knows English pretty well now, and tries to understand all that is said to him."

"Certainly," said Mrs. Rush, "they may all come if they wish, and then we shall not miss Gracie and Lily so much."

VI.

THE SUNDAY SCHOOL.

WHEN Sunday afternoon came they all met as had been arranged, in the lovely nook the Colonel had chosen for them. The little girls were there with Harry, Fred and Hafed. Bob Porter had asked that he might come too. Mrs. Rush was quite willing, but she feared that such great boys would not care for the simple lessons she taught to Maggie and Bessie. She knew they were all too gentlemanly to interrupt or trouble her; but she thought they might grow tired or think it was like babies' play; so she told them they might go if they did not like it.

But she was quite mistaken, for they all, even Bob, who was the oldest, listened not only with respect and attention, but also with great interest, and joined in the lessons with the best of good will.

Frankie was there too, for he had begged to come, and had been allowed to do so on the promise that he would behave very well and sit still. Sitting still was even harder work for Frankie than it was for Maggie; but he meant to be good and quiet, and would probably have kept his word if he had not been troubled. For by and by they all found that even in this quiet nook they were not to remain undisturbed.

Frankie sat as far as possible from Bob, with whom he was much displeased, though he had no good reason to be so. A short time before this, the little ones had all been playing on the grass in front of the house, while the grown people sat upon the piazza. It would have been thought that it was not easy for any one of them to get into mischief or danger with so many to watch them; but Frankie had a way of doing this which was quite surorising. Never was such a fellow for climbing as that Frankie, and his neck was in danger half a dozen times a day, in spite of all the care that could be taken. His mother's eye had been off of him for scarcely two minutes, when she was startled by hearing Maggie say in a terrified voice, " Oh, mamma, do come to Frankie !"

At the side of the house, and just beyond the end of the piazza stood the old well, which supplied them with fresh, cool water. There was a high stone curb around it through which ran a wooden spout, which carried off any waste water which might be poured from the bucket. This spout was partly outside, partly inside the well, and sloped towards the ground. The children, who wanted a drink, had run around to the well, and were waiting for some one to come and draw water for them, when Frankie climbed upon the spout, and before his sisters could stop him, perched himself astride the well curb. Mrs. Bradford turned her head at the sound of her little daughter's voice, and saw them both holding Frankie, the one by his skirts, the other by his leg, while the child was struggling in a frantic manner to free himself from their hold. Had he done so, he must surely have fallen into the well. Before any of the startled group upon the piazza could reach him, Bob Porter darted from the kitchen door, and snatching the child from the well curb, carried him, still struggling, to his mother. Mrs. Bradford thought it best to punish Frankie, and tying the mischievous little feet together with papa's pocket-handkerchief, she made him sit quiet upon the piazza steps for half an hour. When she let him go, he promised to do so no more but he was not reasonable; and instead of being sorry for his own naughtiness, was angry with Bob, who had carried him to his mother, and who, he thought, had caused him to be punished; and now he would not come near him or speak to him, which amused Bob very much.

When the children had all taken their

places, and had done expressing their delight at the pleasant place in which they found themselves, Mrs. Rush opened the school; while the Colonel with his book stretched himself upon the rocks above, until he should be called upon for his accustomed story.

Every child then repeated a hymn, except Hafed, who could not yet master enough English for this, after which Mrs. Rush asked each one for a Bible verse.

"Can you say a pretty verse for me, Frankie?" she asked of the little boy who had just seen a fish throw himself out of the lake, and was eagerly watching for a second glimpse of him.

"Yes 'm. Dat's a pollywod, I dess," said Frankie, with his eyes on the water.

"That's a great Bible verse," said Fred, beginning a giggle, in which the other boys could not help joining.

"Hush, Fred," said Mrs. Rush. "What was that nice verse I heard mamma teaching you this morning, Frankie?"

"Suffer 'ittle chillens — dat *is* a pollywod, Fred — suffer 'ittle chillers to tome unto me;" said Frankie.

"And who said that, Frankie?"

"Jesus," answered Frankie, bringing his eyes back from the lake to the face of his teacher, and becoming interested. "Jesus said it, and it means me."

"Yes, it means you, Frankie."

"And Maddie and Bessie," said Frankie.

"And all other little children," said Mrs. Rush.

"Not Bob," said Frankie, with a defiant shake of his head at the big boy, who had to put his hand over his face to hide the smile which would have way.

"Yes, and Bob, too. Jesus meant all children whoever they may be, or wherever they are."

"But Bob is naughty," said Frankie. "He telled mamma to tie my foots."

"Bob is very good, and Frankie must not be angry with him," said Mrs. Rush. "Frankie was naughty himself, and so mamma had to tie his little feet so that he might remember he was not to run into mischief."

"Jesus don't love naughty boys," said Frankie, with another reproving look at Bob.

"Jesus loves all children, the good ones and the naughty ones," said Mrs. Rush. "It makes him sorry when they are naughty and forget what he tells them, but he still loves them, and wants them to come to him and learn to love him, and be sorry for their sins."

"Did Jesus say I was naughty when I wode on the well?" asked Frankie.

"Did you not know mamma did not want you to climb on the well?" said Mrs. Rush.

"Yes'm; mamma said 'don't do by de well,' and I did do dere."

"And Jesus says little boys must mind their mothers; so he was sorry when he saw Frankie disobey his kind mamma."

"Is he sorry wis me now? I not do so any more," said Frankie.

"He is sorry if you are cross, and do not feel pleasant to Bob," answered Mrs. Rush.

Frankie jumped down from his seat, and running over to Bob, put up his rosy lips for a kiss, which the other was quite ready to give.

"Aunt May," said Maggie, "do you think Jesus *could* love children like Lem and Dolly?"

"He loved them so much that he came to die for them, Maggie. If he did not love them, he would not grieve to see them going so far from him; and to them, too, he says, 'Come unto me,' and stands ready to forgive them, and make them his own little lambs."

"Perhaps they never heard about Jesus, and do not know that he loves them," said Bessie. "I don't believe they have any one to teach them."

"I am afraid not," said Mrs. Rush. "Perhaps some time one of us may find a way to tell them."

"They would not let us speak to them," said Maggie.

"If we could persuade them that we felt kindly to them, they might listen to us," said Mrs. Rush; "at least, we could try."

"But I don't think I do feel kindly to them," said Maggie, "and even if I did, I do not see how we could find the chance to show it."

"I do not say that you will, only that you *may* find it," said Mrs. Rush; "but if you have a chance and do not take it, it will be a jewel by the way which you will not stoop to pick up that you may carry it to your Father in Heaven."

"And Benito would not have passed it by," said Maggie softly. "We will try to be like him, will we not, Bessie?"

When the proper time came, the Colonel was called upon and came down among the children. His story proved even more interesting than usual; and all, from Mrs. Rush down to Bessie, were so taken up with it, that they were not thinking of Frankie, who for some time sat quiet between his little sisters, busy with the Colonel's pencil-case and a piece of paper, on which he was making scrawls which he called "pollywods." He had seen some pollywogs, or young frogs, in the brook the day before, and his mind had been quite full of them ever since; and he was very anxious to catch one, and have it for his own.

Suddenly all were astonished by a loud sob and a half angry, half frightened "stop dat" from the little boy; and looking at him, they saw him with flushed cheeks, quivering lips, and eyes swimming in tears, gazing up at the bushes which overhung the rocks.

"What is it, dear?" asked Mrs. Rush; and as she spoke Maggie and Bessie both caught sight of a hideous face which thrust itself with a threatening look from among the leaves.

"Somebody bad and ugly, he mates faces at me," said Frankie, with another sob.

"It's Lem; I know it is," said Maggie; "and he is making such horrid faces."

All looked up. No face was to be seen, for it had been drawn back; but at that instant down came a shower of sticks, stones and dried leaves, and the loud, taunting laugh they had heard before, rang out from above.

This was too much for the patience of the boys; even cool-headed, steady-going Harry started to his feet in a rage; and he, Bob and Hafed rushed out of the cleft, while Fred, who still had to move slowly, was only kept from following by the Colonel's express commands.

Colonel Rush was out of patience himself, but he knew it would only make bad worse for the boys to get into a fight; and he would not suffer Fred to go, and called loudly on the others to return.

In the heat of the chase they did not hear him, but he need not have feared. Lem and Dolly had no mind to be caught, and were off before the boys reached the top of the steps. Lem ran like a hare, and was out of sight among the trees in an instant; while Dolly, finding the boys were gaining upon her, threw herself upon the ground when she came to the brow of a steep hill, and rolled over and over until she reached the foot, not heeding the stones which must have hurt and bruised her as she went. This had its droll side, and the three boys stood above and laughed as they watched her, though Harry almost feared she would break her neck. But she reached the bottom in safety, and jumping to her feet with a loud whoop of defiance, darted away among the thick woods of the ravine, and was gone.

When the boys came back, the Colonel and Mrs. Rush tried to have the children all settle down quietly again; but the little ones were uneasy and disturbed, starting at every sound, — the twitter of a bird, the splash of a fish, or the dropping of a leaf, — and the Colonel, seeing this, hastened to bring his story to a close, and take them back to the house.

When Mr. Porter heard of the new trouble at the hands of Lem and Dolly, he said they had no right to be there, for it was his ground, and he should see it did not happen again, for he would not have his boarders disturbed. He told Colonel Rush they had better take the house-dog, old Buffer, with them the next Sunday, and let him watch on the rocks above, so that no one could come near. Buffer was a wise dog, and if put on guard, he would not leave his post till he was told he might; so now the children felt they would be safe in their "Sunday bower," as they called the cleft in the rock.

When Mrs. Bradford went up stairs with her children at their bed time, she always read a chapter from the Bible to Maggie and Bessie, and this night she chose the fifth chapter of Matthew. She had no especial thought of Lem and Dolly Owen when she did so; but as she finished, Maggie said, —

"Mamma, don't you think Lem and Dolly 'despitefully use us, and persecute us?'"

"Yes, dear, I think they do," answered mamma, taking pains not to smile.

"I am sure they do," said Maggie. "I do not know if any one could do it worse; for we never did a thing to them."

"Then you know what you are to do for

them," said mamma. "It was our Saviour himself who said these words, 'pray for them which despitefully use you and persecute you.' If we could do nothing else, there is still this left to us."

"And could that be a jewel by the way which we might carry to our Father in heaven, mamma?" asked Maggie.

"Yes, love, indeed it would be," said her mother, thinking as she spoke of Bessie's heartfelt prayer for the miserable children a few nights since, and sure that it would indeed prove a jewel bright and lovely in the eyes of Him to whom it was offered.

Maggie's face looked as if her little head was full of grave thoughts, and she went to bed more soberly than usual, whispering to Bessie as she lay down,—

"We'll take up the jewel of prayer, any way, wont we Bessie?"

Dear little pilgrims! there were jewels in their way such as they did not dream of; but it was only earnest seeking such as theirs which could find them; for they lay hidden beneath many a thorn and bramble and unsightly weed; and they were to be found only by the help of this very jewel of prayer which shone so brightly that its light guided the little feet to the dark places where the hidden gems lay

VII.

THE SILVER CUP.

DAY after day passed by at Chalecoo and each one seemed to bring some new happiness. A book could be filled in telling all the children did in this charming place, of the drives they took in the great rockaway, of their rows upon the lake, of their walks in the lovely woods and glens, and even of one or two wild clambers over the higher rocks where the little girls had to be helped up and down, and Bessie often to be carried in the arms of papa or Uncle Ruthven. Sometimes, however, the grown people and boys went on expeditions which Mrs. Bradford thought too fatiguing, or hard, for her little girls, and they staid at home with grand-mamma and Colonel and Mrs. Rush; for the startled at the thought that Lem had been so near them, and still more frightened by Fanny's excitement, Bessie burst into a loud passionate cry.

"Oh! make him give it back," she said. "It's mine; it's my very own cup that Aunt Bessie gave me. I *will* have it; the bad, bad boy. Oh! make him give it back, Fanny.'

Maggie threw her arms about her, and she, too, burst into tears.

"Come, we'll send some one after him," said Fanny, springing down from the rocks and forgetting her open dairy; leaving butter, cream cheese, all, just as it stood, she seized a hand of each frightened child, and they ran towards the house as fast as Bessie's small feet could go.

Mrs. Bradford was not a little startled when they rushed in upon her, all three excited and out of breath; and Bessie sprang into her arms with another outbreak of cries and exclamations.

As soon as they discovered the cause of the

trouble, Mr. Bradford, Mr. Stanton, and Mr. Porter's oldest son started for the "Chief's Head" to see if they could find the supposed thief and recover the lost cup.

VIII.

A KIND WORD FOR LEM.

THE path up the mountain could be plainly seen from below for nearly half its length; then it was often hidden by many a sharp turn and corner, or the trees and bushes which bordered it on either side. As John Porter and the two gentlemen stood at its foot and gazed upward, they could see nothing of Lem; and they went on cautiously, looking from side to side lest he should be hiding among some one of the many nooks and crannies of the rocks. But they did not find him till they reached the very crown of the " Chief's Head," where they came upon him lying full length upon his back beneath the shade of a pine-tree, eating an apple.

They had mounted so quietly that not even his quick ear had heard them till they were close upon him, and he caught sight of John Porter turning a corner of the rock. Then he sprang to his feet, and, with a guilty but fierce look, darted around so as to bring the pine-trees between him and his pursuers.

But there was no chance of escape on this bare, high point of the mountain. To throw himself down, or go rushing and scrambling over the rocks and every thing else that lay in his way, as he would have done in another place, would not do here, where a false step or a slip would carry him to certain death; and, in a moment, John Porter had his hand upon his collar, and giving him a rough shake, ordered him to give up the cup.

"What cup? I aint got no cup," answered Lem.

"None of that; give it up now," said John, and plunging his hand several times into Lem's pockets, he brought out, no silver cup, but half a dozen large bough apples.

"My own Osborn apples!" exclaimed John, quite forgetting the cup at this sight. "I'd know them anywhere. The rascal must have stripped the tree, and it is the first year it has borne. I set so much store by them! I'll fix you for this," and John gave his prisoner two or three hard cuffs.

"Stop, John," said Mr. Bradford, "that is not the way to deal with him;" and speaking gently but firmly to Lem, he told him that if he would tell where the cup was to be found he should not be punished so severely as if he still continued to keep it concealed.

But the boy still declared he knew nothing of any cup; and, after hunting in vain for it among all the clefts of the "Chief's Head," they had to give up the search. There were a thousand places on the way up where he might have hidden it, and it was useless to look without some clew.

So, having picked up his beloved apples, John Porter led his prisoner down the mountain, followed by Mr. Bradford and Mr. Stanton. They had nearly reached the end of the path, when Dolly suddenly appeared upon it. She was about to start aside, and either run or hide herself, after her usual fashion, when her eye fell upon Lem in John Porter's grasp. Now Dolly had heard nothing of the cup, but she knew that Lem had meant to rob John Porter's tree of its tempting fruit, and she was on her way to meet him at the "Chief's Head," according to his bidding, and have a share of the ill-gotten prize. When she saw him, she supposed that John had taken him prisoner for stealing his apples; and Lem had too often before been in such trouble for her to think it a very serious matter. She did not look for any thing worse, as the consequence of this wickedness, than a whipping, or perhaps that he should be shut up for a few hours; and, although she scowled angrily at her brother's captors, she said nothing to them or to him, but turned and followed at a little distance.

When they reached the house, Mrs. Bradford came out, and begged her husband and brother not to be too hasty in making up their minds that Lem had stolen the cup. For, when they had started to go after the boy, it was supposed that Fanny had seen him take it, but it appeared she had not.

Fanny, though kind and good-natured, was not a very wise young woman; and when she had rushed into the house in such an excited manner, she said that she had put the cup on the shelf of the little window, that Lem had come over the rocks at the back of the dairy, put his hand in at the window, snatched out the cup, and run up the mountain with it.

Now Fanny fully believed that Lem had done all this; but she did not *know* that he had, for she had not seen him. Wicked boy though she knew him to be, she would not have willingly accused him of that of which he was not guilty; but she had spoken as if she knew it to be so, and the two gentlemen, thinking there was no time to lose if the cup was to be recovered, had at once set out after the supposed thief.

But when Maggie and Bessie had been quieted and questioned, their answers showed that no one of the three had seen the cup go; but when they missed it, they had gone out to look for it behind the dairy. Then Fanny, noticing the traces on the rocks, and next seeing Lem climbing the mountain-path, had at once concluded that the bad boy must be the thief.

Next it came out there was another person who might have made his way to the back of the dairy and stolen the cup, and this was the man with the pack on his back, whom they had all three seen going down the lake road. This proved to have been a pedler, who had been up to the house, and whom Mrs. Porter, who never suffered such people about, and who did not like the man's looks, had warned off the place.

Still, every one believed that Lem had been the thief. The boy stoutly and fiercely denied it; and Dolly, when she heard of what he was accused, went into a violent rage, crying and screaming, and threatening, if he was not allowed to go, all manner of revenge, especially against the children, whom she seemed to think were chiefly to blame for this. Mrs. Bradford and the other ladies tried to comfort the poor, desolate child; but she would suffer no one to come near her, cursing and striking about her in a way which made every one fear to approach her. Mrs. Porter carried her some dinner, but she threw it in the kind old lady's face, and then ran off as fast as she could. Mr. Porter sent Bob and one of his older brothers to search once more for the lost cup, and John Porter went down to the village to see if he could find any trace of the pedler.

Meanwhile Mr. Porter said he should shut Lem up until the next morning: a punishment which he deserved for the theft of the apples, which he could not deny, since they had been found upon him, and the tree was entirely stripped.

"Maybe it was that which frightened him, and made him look so guilty when you came upon him," said Mr. Porter; "I am sure, bad and troublesome as he is, I hope it may be so."

"I wasn't scared, neither," said Lem, sullenly; "takin' a few apples aint no great; but I knowed for sure they was after me for some harm. Nobody ever comes after Dol and me for no good."

Though this was said in a sulky, defiant way, there was something in the speech which went straight to Bessie's tender little heart. Perhaps it also touched more than one grown person there, and made them wish, more earnestly than before, that they might do something for these two poor, neglected children.

But Mr. Porter was no hard jailer. Lem was taken to a little disused tool-house, where he was locked up, and one of the hired men put on guard outside, so that he might do no mischief; Mr. Porter having first provided him with a good meal, if he chose to eat it.

A Kind Word for Lem.

"Maggie," said Bessie to her sister that afternoon, "did you hear what Lem said when Mr. Porter spoke about his being frightened when papa and Uncle Ruthven found him?"

"Yes," said Maggie, "and it made me very sorry for him, and that thing came into my throat that comes when you want to cry, and you're afraid some one will ask what you are crying about."

"I wonder if we could not do something to show him we would like to be kind to him," said Bessie.

"But he is shut up," said Maggie.

"Yes; but you know that there is a pile of logs by the window of that little house, and we could get up on it and speak to him, and let him know we would like to come near him to do him good. We'll go and tell him we will ask Mr. Porter to let him out if he will promise not to steal any more."

"Yes," said Maggie, "Mr. Porter said he would do any thing for me for my birthday that I asked him, if it was reasonable; and I s'pose he wouldn't mind doing it a little before, and I think this is pretty reasonable, don't you, Bessie?"

"Yes, and that's a very nice idea of you, Maggie," said Bessie; and this being agreed upon, they went off together.

The pile of logs which lay at the side of the tool-house was not hard to climb, and they had more than once played upon it with their brothers, and now they mounted upon it, and put their two little faces close to the wooden bars which crossed the small window. It was growing late, and the tool-house was rather dark, but they could just see the boy's figure as he sat all in a heap upon the floor. As the little light which came through the bars was partly darkened by the two small faces, he started up, saying roughly, "Clear out now!"

At this, Maggie ducked, fearing she scarcely knew what; but Bessie, though she also was rather frightened, held her ground, and said, gently, —

"We want to speak to you, Lem."

"None of your speaking. Be off with you, will you?" said the boy, looking around for something he might throw at the window.

But there was nothing on which he could lay his hands. Mr. Porter had taken care to carry off every thing which could possibly be turned to mischief.

"But we are going to do you a favor," said Bessie.

"I want none of your favors; let me alone now," answered Lem.

"But we are going to do it to you whether you think you want it or not," said Bessie; "'cause you *will* be glad of it. We are going to ask Mr. Porter to let you out. Will you promise not to steal any more, Lem?"

"I didn't touch your cup," said Lem.

"Well, maybe you did not," said Bessie; "I'd rather think you did not. I'd rather think it was the pedler-man."

"Much you'd care who took it, if you once got it back," said the boy, sulkily.

"But I would care, and so would Maggie,"

said Bessie. "I'd rather — yes — I think I would — I'd rather be sure you hadn't taken it and never find it, than to find it and know you did steal it. Yes, I would, Lem, and I do love my cup very much."

"Oh! come now," said Lem, "you aint goin' to make me say I took it by any of that cant. Are you goin' or not?" and he came closer to the window, with a threatening look.

"We'll go in a minute," said Bessie. "This is my Maggie," and she put her arm about the neck of her sister, who had summoned up courage to peep in at the window again. "Pretty soon she is going to have a birthday, and Mr. Porter said he would do any thing she asked him for, and so she is going to ask him to do it for her now, and to let you out. Will you be glad of that, Lem?"

"You aint a goin' to make me say I took your old cup," persisted Lem, with some very bad words; and, too much shocked to talk to him any more, the little girls slipped down from the logs and ran away.

But shocked and frightened though they were, they did not forget their kind purpose; and a couple of hours later, Mr. Porter unlocked the door of the tool-house. His son John stood by, a lantern in his hand.

"I am going to let you out," said Mr. Porter to Lem; "not that you deserve it, if it was only on account of the apples, and I did mean to keep you here till to-morrow night at least; but those dear little girls that you've plagued so, have begged you off, and I couldn't refuse them. So just you bear that in mind, my lad, and let them alone for the time to come, or you won't find me so easy when next you fall into my hands. Here," and Mr. Porter put a package of food into the boy's hands, "take this, and be off with you. My son will see you safe home; for it's an awful dark night, and you might break your neck on the rocks without a light."

Had Lem done as he wished, he would have rushed off without waiting for company or light; but it was a terribly dark night, not a star was to be seen, for the whole sky was covered with the black clouds which told that a storm was coming, and he knew well enough that he could never find his way home over those dangerous rocks, without the light of the lantern. John Porter, though a good-natured man, was not at all pleased that his father had let Lem off so easily. The loss of the first of his much-prized Osborn apples, while they were yet half-ripe, had vexed him sorely, and he would have liked that Lem should have been severely punished for that theft, even had he not, in common with the rest of the household, believed that he had stolen the silver cup.

So, although he had agreed to his father's wish that he should see the boy safely over the most dangerous part of his way home, he did it with no good-will, and trudged along in silence, turning over in his mind whether or no he could resolve to let Lem go without giving him a good thrashing. But he had been in the kitchen that evening, when Maggie and Bessie had gone to the porch to speak to his father for Lem, and he had heard all that had passed; and now, as he remembered how sweetly and generously the two dear little girls had pleaded for the boy who had treated them so badly, he could not resolve to give him even a part of the punishment he so richly deserved.

"The little dears mightn't like it if they knew it," he said to himself, "and I wouldn't like to be outdone in forgiveness by two babies such as they are, so I'll keep my hands off him, though it does go against the grain to do it."

Perhaps Lem guessed something of what was passing in John Porter's mind, for he took good care to keep beyond the reach of his powerful arm until they reached the miserable hovel which served him for a home.

"Well," said John, raising his lantern so as to throw its light within the crazy door, "this is a pleasant kind of a place to pass such a night as this is like to be. I'm thinking you'd have done better in our old tool-house, my lad. Where's t'other one?" meaning Dol.

"Dunno, and don't care," answered Lem.

"Off on some new mischief, I'll be bound," said John. "Well, good-night to you, if you can pass a good night here," and he walked away, in haste to be home before the storm should break.

Dol was, alas! in some new mischief, — mischief such as John did not dream of; or, although the gust swept through the forest and over the lake, and the rain poured heavily down just as he set his foot upon the threshold, he had not gone so quietly to his mother's sitting-room, and read the paper aloud to her, as she knitted away on his next winter's stockings.

IX.

DOL'S REVENGE.

LEM had told John Porter he did not know and did not care where Dol was on that dark night; but he had not told the truth when he said he did not care. He *did* care, for she was the only thing he loved in all the wide world, and had he known where to look, he would certainly have gone in search of her. But, reckless as he was, he knew that a blind hunt over the mountain on such a stormy night would be worse than useless; and he could do nothing but wait patiently as he might till the morning came.

The storm raged all night: the rain poured down in a driving flood; the lightning flashed; the thunder pealed without rest, echoing from one to another of the mountain-peaks in a long, heavy roll; and the wind blew in furious gusts, shaking even Mr. Porter's comfortable, well-built house, and seeming as if it would lay flat the miserable walls of Lem's poor house, so that the boy was afraid to stay within, and sheltered himself as well as he could beside the rock.

He was troubled about his sister. In all their freaks, in all their wicked doings, they generally kept together, and stood by one another, and he had expected to find her in the hovel when he returned to it that evening He knew well enough that no one would care to take her in for the night; for, if they did so, they were sure to suffer for it before she left the place which had given her shelter. He waited till an hour or so after daybreak, when the storm was dying away, and was just setting out to look for her, when he saw her coming wearily up the little wood-path.

Accustomed as he was to her miserable appearance, even Lem was struck by the wretched plight she was in. The water was dripping from her uncombed, tangled hair and poor rags; her face was pale, and her bare arms and knees were cut and bleeding; and, although the morning was clearing up close and warm, she shivered and drew herself together as if she were suffering from cold. But the wan, haggard face lighted up for a moment when she saw her brother, and she exclaimed,—

"Oh! Lem, did you cheat 'em, and break out?"

"No," said Lem, "he le'me out; and Dol, I say, it was all along of those two little gals They said they'd beg me off, and the old man said they did, and I aint goin' to trick 'em no more. Where was you last night?"

"In the Ice Glen," answered Dolly.

Lem gave a long, astonished whistle.

"You aint goin' to say you slept in the Ice Glen?"

"I didn't do no sleepin', but I was there all night, after I come away from Porter's. But I fixed 'em down there fust," she added with a malicious grin.

"But how came you into the Ice Glen; didn't you know better?" asked Lem.

In answer, she told him how she had been hanging about Mr. Porter's grounds till long after dark, when the storm broke, and she had lost her way; and, after one or two bad falls, had found herself in the Ice Glen; that, knowing the danger in the darkness of a fall over the rocks or into the lake, she had remained there all night, fearing to move till there was sufficient daylight to show her the way home.

"And what was you doin' to keep you down to Porter's so long?" asked Lem.

The reply to this question, instead of being received with praise and exclamations of triumph as she had expected, was met by a curse; and poor Dol shrank down in fear of a blow; for, though Lem was not often angry with her, when he was, she was used to feeling the weight of his hand. But he did not strike her now, but turned sullenly from her, and began trampling down the wet grass with his bare feet.

"What's come over you, now?" she asked at last.

"Nothin'. 'Taint no odds," he answered.

"Aint you glad I fixed 'em off so?"

"No: 'twant fair after they begged me off."

"They got you shut up first, sayin' you took the cup when you didn't."

"How do you know I didn't?"

"'Cause I know who did."

"Did you?"

"No, but I know who did; and what's more, I know where it is now," she answered.

"Tell me then."

But Dolly turned sulky in her turn, and refused to say a word more; and Lem, knowing it was useless to try to make her speak when she did not choose, strolled into the woods to see if he could find any berries for his breakfast; while she, still shivering from her night's exposure in the Ice Glen, tried to kindle a fire from the wet sticks which lay around; and finding this in vain, crept to her wretched bed, and tried to warm herself there.

But it is time to tell what was the new piece of mischief by which Dolly had thus brought punishment upon herself.

Two little pairs of feet danced through the hall, and out upon the piazza of the Lake House that morning.

"Oh, what a nice, pleasant day after the rain!" said Bessie. "The birdies are singing so to tell us how they like it."

"And it is so nice and cool after all the heat," said Maggie. "See! see! papa, how the rain-drops are hanging on the leaves, and how the sun shines in them and makes them sparkle. But what a lot of leaves are lying about over the grass! and there is a branch broken and hanging down."

"There is another lying by the well," said Bessie, "and those large bushes are all leaning over. Did the rain do that, papa?"

"The wind did it," said papa. "The storm was very severe last night, and I fear it may have done some harm to the farm and garden."

"Not to our gardens, I hope," said Maggie. "They looked so nicely yesterday, and Cousin Alexander is coming up to-day to see them; and if the storm did hurt them, we won't have time to fix them up again before he comes."

"If my garden was mussed up a little bit, I shouldn't mind it so very much, if only my dear heliotrope is not hurt," said Bessie.

"And my geranium," said Maggie. "We would be too disappointed if any thing happened to those two. Papa, do you know when Cousin Ernest was here the other day, he said not one of the children had such a fine heliotrope or geranium, and he thought they were sure to take prizes? and besides, he said our gardens were so neatly kept it was a pleasure to look at them."

"Yes," said papa: "you have been very industrious and persevering, and deserve much praise. Here comes Mr. Porter."

"What a terrible night it has been," said Mrs. Bradford, coming out at that moment. "I could not sleep for the noise of the thunder and the wind. I wonder what those two forlorn children have done: that wretched hut could be but poor protection on such a night."

"Better than they deserve," growled Mr. Porter, in a tone very unusual with him, coming up the piazza steps as Mrs. Bradford spoke. "Good-morning, madam. A bad night's work this. I've just been round with the boys to see what damage has been done."

"Not much I hope," said Mrs. Bradford.

"Well, not so much from the storm," said Mr. Porter. "The corn is beaten down a little, but it will rise again in a day or two, and some branches here and there stripped off; but there's been worse than the wind and rain abroad last night. Mr. Bradford, I'll speak with you a minute, sir."

Mr. Bradford walked aside with the old man, who said to him in a low voice,—

"There's a sore trouble in store for those little dears, and I hadn't the heart to tell them myself. You'll know best how to do it. Their gardens are all destroyed, root and branch; not a thing left. Their pet plants, the heliotrope and geranium that they set so much store by, are rooted up and torn to bits, not a piece left as big as my hand. And it was not the storm either that did it, but just those wicked children, Lem and Dolly, or one of them. I don't think it could have been the boy, for I don't see how he could have found his way down here again last night after John saw him home; but, alone or together, the girl has had a hand in it for sure. John picked up a dirty old sunbonnet she used to wear, lying right in Bessie's garden, and he says she was not at home when he went up with Lem last night. She's done it out of revenge for his being shut up, and I wish Buffer had caught her at it, so I do. My patience is quite at an end, and I'll have them routed out of that place, and sent off somewhere, as sure as my name is Thomas Porter."

Mr. Bradford was very much troubled, for he knew how greatly the children would be distressed; and, as the breakfast-bell rang just then, he said he should not tell them till the meal was over, or no breakfast would be eaten by Maggie or Bessie. He could scarcely eat his own as he watched the bright faces of his two little daughters, and thought what a different look they would wear when they heard the bad news.

It was as he had feared: their grief was distressing to see, all the more so when they found who had done this injury to them. Their father had wished to keep this secret, but they begged so to go and see the gardens, that he thought it best to take them and let them know the worst at once; and they were so astonished when they saw the utter desolation of their own beds, and the difference between them and those which lay around, and asked so many questions, that he was obliged to tell them.

The two brothers, with Hafed and Bob, were already on the spot, spades and rakes in hand, to see what could be done; but, alas! there was little or nothing.

It was indeed sad to see the ruin of what had, but yesterday, looked so neat and pretty. The tiny fences were pulled up, and scattered far and wide; lady-slippers, mignonette, verbenas, and all the other simple flowers which had flourished so well, and given such pride and delight to the little gardeners, were rooted up and trampled into the earth; and, worse than all, the beloved heliotrope and geranium were torn leaf from leaf and sprig from sprig, while their main stems had been twisted and bent, till no hope remained that even these could be revived.

The boys' gardens had suffered some, but not so much as those of the little girls; whether it was that Dolly fancied Maggie and Bessie had been the most to blame for Lem's imprisonment, and so chose first to revenge herself on them; whether it was that their gardens lay nearer to her hand and she had been interrupted in her wicked work before she had quite destroyed the boys', — could not be known.

The grief of the children was pitiful to see. Bessie's could not find words, but she clung about her father's neck, and sobbed so violently that he feared she would be ill, and carried her back to the house to see if mamma could not comfort her. Maggie's was not less violent, but it was more outspoken, and she said and thought many angry things of Lem and Dolly, as she gathered up the bruised leaves and stalks of her own geranium and Bessie's heliotrope. The boys were quite ready to join her in all, and more than all, that she said.

"What are you going to do with that, pet?" asked Uncle Ruthven, coming down to see the ruin, and finding Maggie sitting on an upturned flower-pot, her hot tears still falling on the remains of the two favorite plants.

"Oh! Uncle Ruthven!" sobbed poor Maggie, "I could not bear to see them lying there in the mud and dirt. It seems to me 'most as if they were something live, and we were *so* fond of them. I don't think I can bear it. And, oh! I am so sorry we asked Mr. Porter to let Lem out, just so he could do this, — the bad, wicked boy!"

"I do not think it was Lem's doing, dear," said Mr. Stanton; and then he told Maggie how John Porter had taken Lem home last night just before the storm began, and that it was scarcely possible that the boy could have made his way back in the darkness and worked all this mischief.

"Well, it was Dolly, then," said Maggie; "and I can never, never forgive her: no, never, Uncle Ruthven."

Uncle Ruthven would not argue with her, or try to persuade her to feel less hardly towards Dolly now: he knew it was not the time; the wound was too fresh, the little heart still too sore. Nor did he think it worth while to try and make her forget the trouble yet, but talked to her about it in an interested but soothing manner, till at last he led her back to her mother in a more quiet, gentle mood than he had found her.

Meanwhile the boys had all four set to work

with a good will to try what they could do to make the poor gardens look somewhat less forlorn. It was too late in the season to think of planting new seeds or roots; and the flowers which had been torn up were too entirely destroyed ever to revive again.

Hafed would have taken up every flower from his own garden and transplanted it to those of his "Missy's," if the other boys had not made him understand that this would be useless, and most of them would only droop and die.

The disordered beds were raked smoothly over; the little fence carefully cleaned from the mud which covered it, and set up again; and all the withered, bruised flowers and leaves carried away. Then came John Porter and his brothers, bringing a dozen or so of flowering shrubs in pots, which were neatly set out, taking from the gardens the desolate look they had worn. Next, some bright lady-slippers, sweet pinks and other late summer flowers were taken up with plenty of earth about their roots so that they might not droop, and they too, were put down in their new home.

When all was done, the little girls were called down to see the improvement that had been made. They thanked the boys very heartily; but, in spite of all the pains that had been taken, the gardens were not the same they had been before, not the work of their own hands, the gardens they had watched and tended for the last six or seven weeks.

"Besides," said Maggie, with a mournful shake of her head, "our own dear heliotrope and geranium are quite gone, so we need not hope for any prize. It is too late now to try with any thing else, and we couldn't expect Cousin Alexander to give us one when we have nothing to show that we have taken care of ourselves."

"I don't know about that," said Fred, "Cousin Alexander came down here this morning; and, although he did not mention the word prize, he said he thought he ought to take into account all you had done, as well as what you might have done, and asked us if we did not agree with him. Of course we said yes; so we shall see what he will do."

But not all the petting and coaxing they received, or all the new amusements provided for them, could make Maggie and Bessie forget their ruined gardens, or recover their usual spirits that day. Indeed it was rather a mournful day for the whole family. The melancholy faces of the two little girls grieved their older friends; and, besides, it was sad to know that children like Lem and Dolly should take delight in such wicked, wanton mischief, and to know that there seemed to be no way to do them good; since they only came near those who were weaker and younger than themselves to do them harm, and ran from those who were older and wiser, in fear of the punishment and reproof their wickedness deserved. Neither by kindness nor severity did it seem possible to reach these poor creatures.

Mr. Porter said that one of the dogs should be fastened in the garden for a few nights, till he should see what might be done about having Lem and Dolly removed to some place where they could give no more annoyance to himself and his boarders.

"My darlings," said Mrs. Bradford that night, when she had gone upstairs with the children, "what are you going to do now?"

"To say our prayers, mamma," answered Bessie, rather surprised at the question.

"What prayers, Maggie?"

"Why, 'Now I lay me,' and 'Pray God bless,' and 'Our Father which art in Heaven,'" said Maggie.

"And when we say 'Our Father,' what do we say about forgiveness?"

"'Forgive us our trespasses as we forgive those who trespass against us,'" said Bessie. "I know what you mean, mamma."

"And so do I," said Maggie; "but I *cannot* do it, mamma, I cannot forgive Lem and Dolly as I want to be forgiven myself, so I think I had better leave out that part of 'Our Father,' to-night. I wouldn't like to pray a story."

"Nor would I wish you to say what you did not feel, dearie, but I should like you to pray that from your heart."

"But I could not, mamma," said Maggie. "Why, we have forgiven Lem and Dolly so often, and it is not a bit of use."

"Do you remember what I was reading to you the other night?" said mamma, "how Peter came to our Lord, and asked Him how often he should forgive his enemy. What answer did Jesus make?"

"He said 'forgive him till seventy times seven,'" said Bessie.

"O mamma!" said Maggie. "I never could do that. I think I could be like Peter, and forgive Lem and Dolly seven times; but every time I do it, it grows harder and harder, and I never could do it by the time it was seventy times seven. That is such a lot! Every bit of forgiveness in me would be used up by that time."

"Our Lord only said 'seventy times seven,' to show that we must forgive a great number of times, Maggie. He did not mean to measure our forgiveness any more than He measures His own. He is ready to pardon all who go to Him, as often and as freely as they need. But we must ask Him from our hearts; and can we do so if those hearts are full of unkindness and hard feeling towards those who have injured us? I know how hard it is for you both, my darlings; I know by my own feelings how hard it is to forgive Lem and Dolly; but I cannot hope to be forgiven myself for what I have done wrong this day, unless I forgive them the harm they have done to me."

"They did not harm you, mamma, did they?" asked Maggie.

"Yes: they hurt my two little blossoms, Maggie and Bessie, and so grieved me very much. But I can hope my flowers will soon get the better of the harm they have received; not only of their sorrow, but also of their anger and hard feeling towards those poor, unhappy children. Suppose you had at this moment a chance to do a kind thing, or speak a kind word to Lem and Dolly, — would either of you do it?"

"Mamma," said Bessie, "I think I would. It would be very hard, and I'm afraid I wouldn't quite like to do it; but I would try to think how often Jesus forgave me, and I would say, 'forgive me my trespasses' as I forgive Lem and Dolly, and maybe that would make it easier."

"It will indeed, my darling; and what does my Maggie say?"

"I'll try too, mamma — but — but — I can't help thinking I'd be pretty glad if the chance never came."

X.

THE BANANAS.

"ADDIE," said Frankie, running up to his sister the next morning with a pair of worsted reins in his hands, "will oo fis my weins?"

"Pretty soon, Frankie: I'm busy now," answered Maggie.

"Oo're not: oo're doin' nossin' but sittin'," said the little boy. "Do it now."

"Yes; I am in a meditation, and you must not interrupt me," said Maggie, with a solemn, important face.

Frankie walked round and round her on every side, looking curiously at her, and peering down at her; then said, —

"I don't see it, Maddie."

"Don't see what?" asked Maggie.

"Dat sing oo are in," replied Frankie.

"He means that meditation you said you were in," said Bessie.

At this Maggie laughed merrily, and all her meditations were put to flight.

"O foolish child!" she said. "I s'pose he thought a meditation meant a kind of a thing you could see."

"Maggie," said Bessie gravely, "if you laugh at Frankie, you'll have to laugh at me too, 'cause I don't know what a meditation means either."

"It means," said Maggie, arranging Frankie's reins for him, "to be thinking about whether a thing is right or wrong, and to be trying to make up your resolution to do something that you know you ought to do, but that you don't want to do."

"Oh!" said Bessie in a very satisfied tone; "then I know what you was having a meditation about. And how did you make up your resolution, Maggie?"

"Oh! just to forgive Lem and Dolly without any more fuss about it," said Maggie. "But for all that, Bessie, I would like never to hear or see or think or know or dream any thing more about those two children."

"Who would like to go and play in the woods?" asked Harry, coming out to them. "Mamma says we may all go if we choose."

"I will."

"And I."

"I too," came from his two sisters and Frankie.

"Who is going to take care of us?" asked Bessie.

"Jane and Starr," said Harry. "Fred and I could do it well enough; but mamma is afraid of those two ragamuffins, and the Colonel said they would not dare to trouble us if Starr was with us, and he could very well spare him."

"Hurrah!" cried Fred, rushing out of the house. "Papa, Uncle Ruthven, Aunt Bessie, and Aunt Annie are going with us, and we are going to have a grand corn-roasting up in the woods; hurrah! hurrah!" and Fred tossed his cap in the air, and turned two or three somersets on the grass, which Frankie immediately tried to imitate, but only succeeded in tumbling over on his side. He was quite contented with his own performance, however, and said, with a self-satisfied shake of his head, "I somersat mysef fee times."

The party were soon ready, and started off, grandmamma and mamma, Colonel and Mrs. Rush promising to follow by and by when the fire should be made, and the roasted corn nearly ready for eating.

Butter and salt were packed in a tin pail by Mrs. Porter and carried by Hafed, while Starr brought a basket with plates and knives. The corn was to be plucked from a cornfield which they would pass on their way. The spot chosen was at some distance from the house, up in the woods, where a pure, bright spring bubbled up from the rocks, and then went rippling and singing away in one of those hundred mountain streams. Here was a little cleared space among the trees, and a broad flat stone on which the fire was to be built; while two or three great trunks and stumps formed excellent seats, — excellent, that is to say, for those people who had both their limbs left to them, — but the Colonel did not find them quite so comfortable; so Starr slung a camp chair over his arm to have it ready for his master's use when he should come.

When they came to the cornfield, to reach which they had to take rather a roundabout path, each child loaded itself with as many ears of corn as it could carry. Papa and Uncle Ruthven each took an armful too; so, when they were all laid together, there was quite a pile.

"We will want a pretty large fire to roast all that corn," said Bessie; "we'll have to pick up a great many sticks."

Picking up sticks for the fire was not thought hard work, however, but famous fun; and the little ones began to gather them up with a good will. This was by no means the first fire they had built on this very convenient stone: it had seen many a potato-roast and candy-boiling, though this was the first corn-roasting they had had.

But here quite a misfortune happened to Bessie. As she was coming towards the fire-place, with her hands full of dry branches, she tripped and fell her full length directly in the ashes of the old fires. Her father and other friends could not be thankful enough that the match had not yet been put to the sticks which lay ready for lighting; for if the fire had been burning, she must have fallen into the flames and been badly burned.

But her arms and knees were somewhat bruised on the hard rock, and her white dress and apron sadly soiled and black from the ashes.

Now Bessie was a very neat child,— particular about her dress,— and could not bear to have any thing near her that was not quite clean. The little knees and arms could be washed in the stream, and dried on the towel which had been brought; but there was no way of cleansing the blackened clothes, and Bessie was distressed at the thought of passing the whole morning in such a condition.

"Come then, Miss Bessie," said Starr, "I'll just take you over home, where you may have clean clothes put on, and bring you back before the others know you have gone."

Bessie thanked him, and said she would be very glad; and taking her up in his arms, so that they might get over the ground in short time, the good-natured soldier strode away with her.

Mamma was a good deal surprised, and a little startled, to see her Bessie coming back so soon in Starr's arms; but it was presently explained, and the little girl made quite neat and clean again. She was about leaving the house once more with Starr, when she heard Colonel Rush calling her, and ran back to his room.

"Bessie," said the Colonel, "here are half

a dozen bananas, — one a-piece for each of you children, — yourself and Maggie, your three brothers and Hafed. Would you not enjoy them up in the woods?"

"Yes," said Bessie; "but we will save them till you all come, so all our big people can have some too."

"Oh, no! keep them for yourselves," said the Colonel; "your big people all had enough last night, and I kept these out for you, knowing how fond you and Maggie were of them."

Bessie thanked and kissed him, and ran off, giving her prize to Starr to carry for her.

"There's a way by which I can take you back quicker, if you didn't mind being lifted up a steep place in the rocks. It's quite safe: would you like it, Miss Bessie?" said Starr.

Bessie said she would rather go by the shortest way; and Starr struck into a path, if path it could be called, which was quite new to her. But he carried her safely over the rugged way, while she chatted merrily to him.

"Starr," she said, "I'm going to give you a

piece of my banana, 'cause you're so very kind and good to me."

"Thank you kindly, miss," said the man; "but I never eat them, not if a shipful was before me."

"Don't you like them?" asked the little girl.

"No, miss."

"Oh! I like them better than any thing, — I mean better than any thing else to eat," said Bessie; "and I was very much pleased when the Colonel gave me these, 'cause I didn't have one since I came to Chalecoo."

"Then I am glad, too, miss," said Starr, who in the city had often been sent by his master to buy bananas to indulge this favorite fancy of Bessie's. "Now, Miss Bessie, I am just going to put you on top of this great stone, and climb up myself afterwards, and then we'll be but a few rods from where the ladies and gentlemen are."

Just before them was a mass of rock, four or five feet high, which seemed to bar the way;

but lifting Bessie as high as he could, Starr set her safely upon the top, then handing her the bananas began to clamber up himself.

At that moment a slight rustle made Bessie turn her head, and she found herself face to face with Dolly Owen. Before she had time to utter her astonishment and alarm, Starr stood beside her, and he was the first to speak.

"So, you're there, are you?" he said, sternly. "What wickedness are you up to now, I'd like to know?"

Dolly made no answer, but sat with her eyes fixed upon Bessie, or rather upon the tempting bunch of bananas she held in her small hands. The girl was half lying, half sitting upon the ground, her head and shoulders resting against the trunk of a large tree, her face drawn as if she were in great pain. It seemed as if she must have crept into this nook as a hiding-place, for on all sides, save the one by which Starr and Bessie had come, was a thick growth of underbrush, with only a narrow outlet where the bushes had been partly broken down. From beyond this came the sound of gay voices and merry laughter, showing, as Starr had said, that the rest of the party were not far distant. Very lonely and dreary the wretched child looked, lying there with those happy sounds ringing in her ears, telling that others were so much better off, so much happier than she was.

"What's them?" she asked, looking greedily at the bananas.

"Now are you not ashamed to be speaking to the little lady after what you've done?" said Starr. "Those are not for such as you, and you needn't be asking what they are. And look you here, young one, you let me catch you a step nearer the gentlefolks, and I'll let you hear something you won't like. *My* patience is about come to an end."

Still Dolly took no notice of him. Instead of running away, or cowering in fear of punishment, as she generally did when any grown person came near her, she remained crouched, without moving, upon the ground.

"Gi' me one," she said to Bessie.

"Did I ever hear such impudence!" exclaimed Starr, roused out of his usual stiffness; "well, you are the most graceless creature I ever did see. Come on, Miss Bessie, if you please."

But Bessie gently put aside Starr's hand, as he would have led her away.

"Please wait a minute, Starr."

"I say, gi' me one," said Dolly again; "I aint eat nothin' to-day nor yesterday, and Lem's gone away."

It was, indeed, a bold thing for Dolly to ask any thing of one whom she had injured so much; but she was ravenous with hunger, and having no shame, she had no thought save how she might satisfy it.

Bessie stood looking from her to the bananas. Should she give Dolly her own or not? She wanted it very much herself; but she had asked her Father in heaven to let her find some way to be kind to Lem and Dolly, and now was He not answering her prayer? It had been very pleasant to think of sharing the delicious fruit with her own dear friends whom she loved so much, or even of giving a piece to Starr, who was always so kind and good to her; but to give it all to this bad girl who had done so much cruel mischief to her and hers, was another thing.

Perhaps strong, healthy children, who can enjoy whatever is set before them, can have little idea what a piece of self-denial this was to Bessie. She was a delicate child, with a slight appetite which needed some coaxing, and, as she had said to Starr, if there was any one thing which she liked particularly, it was a fine banana.

Yes, she wanted it very much; but there was poor Dolly who wanted it very much too, — who said she had had nothing to eat all day yesterday, who probably had never tasted such a fruit; for she had asked what they were when she saw them, — who, even Bessie's innocent eyes could see, looked very ill. Was not here a chance to "render good for evil;"

to do the kind thing she had said she would do if she could but find the way?

She had a moment's struggle with herself; then, breaking one of the bananas from the stem, she went a little nearer to Dolly and held it out at arm's length, for she feared the mischievous girl too much to go very close to her.

Dolly raised herself slowly and clutched at the banana, but sank back again with a cry of pain.

"Have you hurt yourself, Dolly?" asked Bessie, gently.

Dolly made no answer, but stretched out her hand again for the fruit.

Bessie went a little nearer, and timidly placed it in her hand.

"That's not the way," she said, as the girl greedily bit into the close, tough skin. "You must peel it. I will show you."

Dolly held fast to the banana for a moment, as if she feared Bessie was about to take it back; then, with a wondering look into the sweet, pitiful little face, gave it up.

"Now, don't you be waiting on her, Miss Bessie," said Starr; "you've done more than enough already, to give her your banana. Will you come, miss, and just leave that girl to herself?"

"I think I'd better fix it for her, Starr. She don't know how, and I think there's something the matter with her," said Bessie: and, stripping the peel from the fruit, she placed it once more in Dolly's hand.

"Does something hurt you?" she asked, as the girl moaned again when she moved.

"Yes, I hurts all over," answered Dolly.

"Did you fall down?"

"No, I didn't," mumbled Dolly, with her mouth full.

"Then how did you hurt yourself so much?"

"Dunno," said Dolly, sullenly. But she did know; she knew right well that those terrible racking pains came from that night spent in the Ice Glen. She had a feeling as if Bessie must know it too. "Now just you and that man clear out. I came here first," she muttered.

"Don't fret yourself: your company's not so pleasant, nor your talk so sweet, that the little lady need want more of it," said Starr. "Miss Bessie, my dear, won't you come?"

"Yes," said Bessie, "in a moment," and then, turning again to the girl,— "Dolly, I am very sorry for you."

"Humph," said Dolly, in a tone as if she could not believe this.

"Don't you think I am?" said Bessie.

"I knows better," was the answer she received.

"But I am, Dolly, really. I am very sorry for you, 'cause you have that pain, and 'cause you don't have any one to love you, and take care of you, and teach you. Wouldn't you let me be a little kind to you?"

"If you're so sorry, give me another of them," said Dolly again, looking at the bananas with a greedy eye. She had never tasted any thing so delicious in her life, and the one which Bessie had given only made her more anxious for a second.

Bessie gave a little sigh.

"I would if they were mine," she said; "but they are not, and so I cannot give them to you."

"Be off then. You're glad I ache so; I know you are 'cause I plagued you so."

Starr's patience was at an end; and, lifting his little charge in his arms, he plunged through the opening in the bushes.

"Miss Bessie," he said, "you ought to let that girl alone; she's not fit for you to care for, and it's all kindness thrown away."

Bessie looked very grave and thoughtful.

"Starr," she said, presently, "if she is fit for Jesus to care for, she must be fit for us to care for."

Starr was silenced: he had not another word to say.

When Bessie reached her playfellows, the fire was burning famously; but they had waited to husk the corn till she should come to have her share in that pleasure.

"But where is your banana?" asked Maggie, when her sister divided the Colonel's gift.

"It is gone," answered Bessie.

"Oh!" said Maggie, "why, didn't you wait to eat it with the rest of us? But never mind, you shall have half of mine."

"Let's husk the corn now," said Harry; "we'll have the bananas by and by."

The ears were soon stripped of their green dress and silken tassels, and laid round the fire to roast. Then Bessie told Maggie she wanted to tell her a secret, and drew her a little aside from the others.

"Maggie," she said, "I did not eat my banana; I gave it away."

"Did you?" said Maggie. "That was very good of you, 'cause you're so fond of them. Who did you give it to?"

"To Dolly," answered Bessie.

"To Dolly! that bad thing!" exclaimed Maggie; "where *did* you see her?"

Bessie told how she and Starr had found Dolly, and of what had passed, ending with,—

"I would have given her another banana if any of them had been mine, Maggie; and I thought you would have given her yours too, to show her you wanted to be kind to her, if you only knew about it."

"So I would," said Maggie, "and I wouldn't have cared if you had given it to her. I will let you do just what you choose with any thing of mine, Bessie, and not be a bit provoked."

"But it was not mine, you see," said Bessie, "and I didn't think it would be right when you did not tell me to."

"I'd give it to her now, if I was to see her," said Maggie; "but then we couldn't go and find her, you know. She might do something to us."

"I don't think she could very well," said Bessie. "It hurts her so to move; and her speaking sounds like mine when I have the croup. Starr said he thought she looked very sick. She's just over behind those bushes, and some one could go and take care of us. I think she would be sure we are sorry for her if we took it to her. Shall we ask papa about it?"

Maggie agreed, and papa was called and told the whole story, and of their wish to take the second banana to Dolly.

He thought it over for a moment or two, and then said he would let them take it, and would go with them to see that no harm befell them at Dolly's hands.

XI.

"*GOOD FOR EVIL.*"

DOLLY was found lying in the same spot, and almost in the same position, in which Bessie and Starr had left her; but now she was half asleep.

Thinking she might receive the children's kindness in a better spirit, if there was no older person to look on, Mr. Bradford helped his little daughters through the screening bushes, and then drew back a few steps where he might still watch them, and hear all that passed, but where Dolly could not see him.

At the rustling of the children's footsteps upon the dry leaves and branches, Dolly started and opened her heavy eyes, to see Maggie and Bessie standing hand in hand before her. The old, fierce, defiant look flashed into them for one moment, then died out again before timid Maggie had time to start back and draw her sister with her.

"My Maggie came to bring you her banana," said Bessie, gently. "*I* couldn't give it to you, 'cause it was not mine; but when I told her you didn't have any thing to eat for most two days, she was sorry for you, and said you should have it."

"It's good. I like it," said Dolly, as Maggie, summoning all her courage, stepped slowly towards her and gave her the banana.

"Dolly," said Bessie, "will you believe now that we are sorry for you, and want to be kind to you?"

"I s'pose so," answered Dolly, gruffly, as if she were still half unwilling or unable to believe that they meant what they said.

They stood in silence, watching the half-famished creature as she eat her fruit, then Bessie said, —

"Dolly, why don't you go home?"

"No, I shan't neither, I aint goin' to stir,"

she answered snappishly, with one quick, suspicious glance at the children, and another towards the trunk of the old tree against which she leaned. "I've got a right here, if I've a mind to stay. 'Taint your ground nor Porter's neither."

"Oh, no!" said Bessie, "I did not mean that, only you have such a bad cold, and it hurts you so to move, and these rocks are so hard, I should think you'd be more comfortable in your bed at home."

"Guess my home's a sight more comfortable than these rocks, aint it?" said Dolly, with a grin. "One's about as good as t'other."

"Poor Dolly!" said Bessie, "I wish you had a better home, and some one to care for you and Lem."

"What for? I s'pose you think I wouldn't bother you then."

"I hope you wouldn't," said Bessie; "but I was not thinking about that. It was only 'cause I am so sorry that you don't have a nice home and plenty to eat, and people to love you. But, Dolly, you know Jesus loves you."

"No, he don't neither," was the answer.

"But he does, indeed he does," said Bessie, earnestly; "he loves you all the time, and it makes him sorry when you are naughty; but if you won't do so any more, but will try to love him, he will be glad, and then you will be his own little child, 'cause he says, 'Suffer little children to come unto me,' and he means all children. Mrs. Rush taught us that one Sunday."

"I say," said Dolly, "I could ha' plagued you last Sunday if I'd had a mind to. The old dog wasn't there."

"No: Buffer was sick last Sunday afternoon," answered Bessie. "Did you come by our Sunday bower?"

"I came by the place where you go of Sundays," said Dolly; "but I didn't do nothin', 'cause I had a mind to hear you singin'. It sounded nice: I liked it."

"Will you come next Sunday?" said Bessie, eager for the slightest chance of doing Dolly good. "Mrs. Rush and the Colonel would let you, I am sure; and they'll tell you about Jesus a great deal better than I can, and how he loves you, and will take you to heaven, if you will only be a good girl and love him. Wouldn't you like to hear about it?"

"Dunno," said Dolly; "I like to hear you sing. Jesus is God, aint he?"

"Yes," said Bessie, coming closer to the poor girl, and drawing Maggie with her. "He is God's Son, and he came away from his heaven to die for us, so we could go there, and live with him, if we would only love him and do what he tells us. And heaven is such a beautiful place! Dolly, the angels are there; and every one will be so happy; and no one will be hungry or sick or tired there; and Jesus will take care of us always, always. Wouldn't you like to go there, Dolly?"

"I'd like to go somewhere," said Dolly wearily; "I'm about tired of this. I'd like not to be hungry, nor to have this pain no more. But 'taint likely your Jesus wants me in his beautiful place. I s'pose he wants clean folks with nice clothes, not old dirty rags like mine."

Maggie was beginning to feel braver as she saw that Dolly was quiet and not in a mood for mischief, and now she spoke.

"Jesus won't mind about rags if you only have a heart that loves him," she said. "He loves you just as much in your rags, as he loves some other little girl who is dressed nicely."

"How do you know he loves me?" asked Dolly.

"'Cause the Bible says so," said Maggie; "so it must be true, 'cause the Bible is God's word. And besides, Dolly, if Jesus came to die for you, so you could go to heaven, don't you think he must love you? When a person does a very kind thing for you, don't that make you think they love you?"

"Did you give me them goodies 'cause you loved me?" said Dolly.

Maggie was rather disturbed at this question, and did not know how to answer it; but Bessie, seeing her trouble, spoke for her.

"Why, no, Dolly," she said, "I'm 'fraid we

don't love you very much; you know you couldn't 'spect us to: but we wanted to be kind to you, and to make you know we wanted to forgive you for troubling us so."

"You *was* real good to give me them things," said Dolly; "they was first rate. And you was good to get Lem let out too; he told me. But I say,"—and Dolly really looked half ashamed,—"'twant him did that."

Bessie thought she was speaking of the cup.

"I don't believe very much that he did," she said. "Mr. Porter thinks maybe the pedler-man took it, 'cause he went to Farmer Todd's house, and after he was gone some spoons were lost; and they think he stole them, so maybe he has my cup too."

"I didn't mean that," answered Dolly, slowly. "I meant 'twant Lem spiled your gardens, but —I *am* sorry I done it—there now. And Lem aint got your cup; you can just know it."

"We try to believe he didn't," said Bessie. Then she added, with a quiver of her lip and a tear or two gathering in her eyes, "I don't think *any one* could have taken it if they had known how very fond I was of it. You see, Dolly, I had that cup a great, great many years, ever since I was a little baby; and I always had my drink out of it, so you see we grew up together, and I don't know how I can bear never to see it again. I was pretty much troubled to lose my cup and my garden too."

Dolly looked uneasily at her, moved restlessly on her hard bed, and sank back again with another moan.

"I guess we'll have to go now," said Maggie.

"Will you come next Sunday and hear Mrs. Rush tell about Jesus and how he loved you?" said Bessie. "Or papa and mamma would tell you about it if you liked. They can do it a great deal better than we can."

"No," said Dolly, "I don't want to hear big folks. I don't mind your speaking to me if you choose. But, I say, don't you never sing but on Sundays?"

"Oh, yes!" said Bessie, "we sing every day and sometimes a good many times in the day."

"I like music," said Dolly. "Lem whistles fustrate."

"Yes, we know it," said Maggie. "Once we heard him when we couldn't see him, and we asked Mr. Porter who it was, and he told us it was Lem; and we listened as long as we could hear him: it sounded so sweet and clear. I never heard any one whistle like that."

"Yes," said Dolly, looking pleased; "nobody can beat *him* at that. S'pose you couldn't sing me a tune 'fore you go, could you? It's so lonesome, lying here."

"Why, yes: we will if you want us to," Bessie answered readily, though she as well as Maggie was much surprised at the request. "We'll sing, 'I want to be an angel.'"

So they stood, these two "ministering children," and sang; their young voices rising sweet and clear amid the solemn stillness of the grand old woods; for very still it was. As the first notes arose, the friends whom they had left, hushed laughter and merry talk that they might not lose one of the sweet sounds.

They only knew that Maggie and Bessie had wandered off with papa, and thought this was meant as a pleasant surprise for them.

But it was a higher, greater Friend,—a "Friend above all others,"—whom our little jewel-seekers were just then trying to please; and, although they might not know it, they had that day taken up the first link of the golden chain, by which poor Dolly's soul was to be drawn out of the clouds and darkness in which it had lain, up into the light and sunshine of his glorious presence. A very slight and fragile link it might seem, but it was doubtless very precious in the eyes of the heavenly Father, whose hands could make it strong and lasting, and fit to shine before him in the " day when he shall make up his jewels."

Very precious it was, too, in the eyes of the earthly father, who watched the scene, and looking from his own tenderly cared for, daintily dressed darlings, to the forlorn, ragged outcast, thanked God that for all three alike had the blessed words been spoken, "Suffer little children to come unto me."

"Is that place the song talks about that heaven you was telling about?" asked Dolly when the children had finished "I want to be an angel."

"Yes," said Bessie. "You do want to go there; don't you, Dolly?"

"'Taint no use wantin,'" said Dolly. "I'll never get there, nor Lem neither. Sing some more."

"We'll sing 'Rest for the weary,' 'cause she said she was so tired," said Maggie.

When they were through, Mr. Bradford stepped from behind the bushes which had hidden him until now.

Dolly started when she saw him, and the old look, half guilty, half defiant, came back to her eyes. But she soon found she need not be afraid; for, bending over her, he said, kindly,—

"My poor girl, you are in great pain, I fear. How did you hurt yourself?"

"Didn't hurt myself," grumbled Dolly, still

suspicious, and shrinking from that grave, steady look.

"Then you are ill," said Mr. Bradford, noticing the burning cheeks and heavy eyes, "you must not lie here, or you will be worse. Can you go home?"

"I shan't go home," said Dolly, passionately, and with another quick glance over her shoulder.

Mr. Bradford did not insist, though he meant she should obey him, but said, kindly,—

"Are you still hungry? Would you like some roasted corn?"

Dolly muttered something which might be either no or yes, falling back into her old sullenness; but Mr. Bradford answered as kindly as if she had spoken pleasantly, and told her she should have some.

"Shall we bring it to her, papa?" asked Bessie.

Mr. Bradford said no; for he had been rather startled when he found Dolly was ill, not hurt, as he had first supposed; and he was not willing his little daughters should come near her again, till he was sure what ailed her.

He told the children to bid Dolly good-by, which they did; the girl replying in a more gentle tone than she had yet used, and then calling Bessie back, saying, "Here, littlest one."

But when Bessie looked back to see what she wanted, she refused to speak, and, shutting her eyes, turned her face away.

Mamma and grandmamma, Colonel and Mrs. Rush, had all arrived when our little girls came back to the fire; and the corn was nicely roasted, waiting to be eaten. So the merry, happy party gathered round to enjoy it.

Dolly was not forgotten; for Maggie and Bessie picked out a couple of nice, brown ears, and Starr was sent to carry them to her, — an errand which he did not do very willingly. He came back, saying that he had found her angry, and that she refused to touch or look at the corn.

When all had had enough, Mr. Bradford asked Mr. Stanton if he would go with him and see the poor girl, and tell, if he could, what might be done for her. Uncle Ruthven was not a doctor, but he knew a good deal about medicine, and had often practised it in his travels when no physician was at hand. He willingly agreed to see Dolly, and the two gentlemen went off immediately.

As Mr. Bradford had expected, his brother-in-law pronounced Dolly to be very sick. She would answer no questions, but it was easy to see that she had a bad cold and a high fever, and that the pain, which became so bad when she moved, was rheumatism. Mr. Stanton at once said that she must no longer lie upon the hard, cold rock; she must go home: but it seemed to be doubtful if she could walk. When the gentlemen tried to raise her, they found this no longer doubtful, but quite impossible: the girl's cramped limbs could not hold her up; she could not stir one step. Perhaps she would not have gone had she been able to do so, for she broke forth into angry cries and refusals to be moved, which were only stopped by a violent fit of coughing.

These cries brought the Colonel, with Mrs. Stanton and Starr, to see if they could be of any assistance; and Colonel Rush, finding there was difficulty in moving Dolly, proposed that his camp chair should be brought, and the sick girl carried home in that.

No sooner said than done. Starr was sent for the chair, and when it was brought, Dolly was gently raised and placed in it. She would still have resisted, but she saw that the gentlemen were determined, and it was such agony to move that she thought it as well to submit. When she was in the chair, Mr. Stanton and Starr raised it, and began to move off.

"Wait a bit! wait a bit!" exclaimed Dolly.

"Well, what is it?" asked Mr. Stanton, kindly.

"S'pose I might as well tell," muttered Dolly, as if speaking to herself; "he'll just come back and get it, and I'd liever she'd have it. I say," she added, in a louder tone, "I want to speak to the little gals' pa."

"Well?" said Mr. Bradford, coming nearer.

"You won't say Lem took it, will you?" asked Dolly.

"I would not say Lem took any thing unless I was quite sure of it," said the gentleman.

"Well, then, you just may be sure he didn't take it, and I didn't neither; 'twas the pedler, and I seen where he put it. He didn't know I was behind the bushes, but I seen him. That's why I stayed about, so as to scare him off if he came; but Lem didn't know nothin' about it. I guess I'll tell where he put it, 'cause the little gal was good to me after I plagued her. Jes' you put your hand in that hole, and see what you find;" and, with trembling fingers, she pointed to a hole in the trunk of the old tree against which she had been leaning.

Mr. Bradford put his hand into the opening, and, after feeling about a little, drew forth a bundle. Opening it, he found not only what he had expected to see, Bessie's lost cup, but also Farmer Todd's silver spoons, and one or two other small articles which he thought must have been stolen. The finding of the spoons with the cup, made it almost certain that Lem had not taken the latter; and Mr. Bradford was very glad that he had not suffered appearances to make him judge the boy too harshly.

And now Mr. Stanton and Starr moved on with the chair. They carried it as steadily as possible, but the way was rough, and with all their care every step gave great pain to Dolly. Mr. Bradford and Mrs. Stanton followed to see what could be done to make the poor creature comfortable. Comfortable! that seemed a hopeless task, indeed, when they reached the wretched hovel and looked about them.

Dolly was laid upon the pile of leaves and rags which served for a bed; and Mr. and Mrs. Stanton stayed with her while Mr. Bradford, taking Starr with him, went back to beg from Mrs. Foster what was needful for her.

XII.

UNCLE RUTHVEN'S WORK.

DOLLY, quite tired out with pain, had sunk into a restless sleep; and Mr. and Mrs. Stanton were sitting on the rocks outside the door, waiting till Mr. Bradford should return, when a sweet, clear whistle, like a bird-call, rang through the wood. It was repeated again, and yet again, and was plainly some signal. Each time it came nearer, and at the third sounded close at hand; and the next instant Lem sprang round a point of the rock. As he caught sight of the lady and gentleman before the hovel door, he started, and, after staring at them for one instant, turned to run away.

But Mr. Stanton's voice stopped him.

"Do not run off again," he said, kindly;

"your sister is very sick, and lying here in the house. Come and see her."

Lem stood a moment, half doubtful; then rushed past the gentleman into the house. He came out again presently, his eyes wide open with astonishment and alarm.

"What you been a doin' to her?" he said, fiercely.

"We found her lying upon the rocks, unable to move," said Mr. Stanton, not heeding the angry tone, "and so brought her here in this chair. We have sent to Mrs. Porter for some things to make a bed for her, but no bed can be kept fit for her unless it is quite dry; and I fear this roof of yours is not watertight. I wonder if you and I could not make it so. Do you know where you can buy some straw?"

"Know where there's plenty of straw for them as can pay for it," answered Lem.

"Oh, well," said Mr. Stanton, cheerfully, "you find the straw, and I'll do the paying. There; bring as many bunches as they will give you for that," and he put fifty cents into Lem's hand.

The boy gazed at the money open-mouthed, — probably he had never in his life had so much, honestly come by, in his hands at once, — turned it over, stared at Mr. Stanton, and then again at the money. That any one should trust him with money, or with any thing that had the least value, was something so new that he could scarcely believe his own senses.

"They'll say I didn't come by it fair, and won't give me no straw," he said at last, thrusting the money back upon Mr. Stanton.

The gentleman knew this was only too likely, and too well deserved; and, taking a pencil and slip of paper from his pocket-book, he wrote a few words, and handed the paper to Lem.

Lem could neither read nor write, but he was no fool; and he knew that those few black marks would do more for him than any amount of talking on his own part; but he was even yet a little suspicious. He stood hesitating for a moment, looking back into the house, where his sister lay moaning in her uneasy sleep, then darted away into the path which led down the mountain.

"Do you think he is to be trusted, Ruthven?" said Mrs. Stanton. "Will he come back?"

"I think so," replied her husband; "any way, I thought I would try it. It may give me some hold upon him."

In less time than could have been thought possible by one who knew the distance he had to go, Lem was back; but a good deal had been done in the mean time. Mr. Bradford had returned with Starr and John Porter, bringing a straw bed and pillow, a coarse but clean pair of sheets, and a blanket. Good old Mrs. Porter came too, full of pity for the forlorn, sick child, and carrying a kettle of tea, ready milked and sugared.

The bed had been made, — upon the floor, to be sure: there was no other place to put it,

—Dolly had been given some medicine, her fevered face and hands washed, and she laid in the bed. A fire had been kindled without, and the tea warmed afresh; and when Lem came back with the straw, Mrs. Porter was just offering Dolly a drink. She took it eagerly; but, although she knew Lem, she would not speak to him, and soon sank again into an uneasy sleep or stupor. Lem had brought six bundles of straw; and, throwing them down, he handed Mr. Stanton some change, saying the man from whom he had bought them could let him have no more, and had given him back that money.

Mr. Stanton privately asked John Porter how much the straw should have cost, and found that Lem had brought him the right change. So here was something gained: the boy had been true to his trust for once.

"Now we will go to work," said Mr. Stanton to Lem; and he told him to follow him deeper into the woods, where he soon cut down a dozen or so of tall, slender saplings, and bade Lem strip them of their leaves and branches.

When these were finished, some long strips of birch bark were cut by Mr. Stanton, while Lem stood looking on, and wondering if it were possible the gentleman could be taking so much trouble for him and Dolly, and what in the world he could be going to do with those things. That was soon seen. When all had been made ready and carried to the hut, Mr. Stanton made Lem climb upon the low roof, and, directing him how to lay the straw so as to cover the worst part, bound it in its place with the saplings, and tied them down with the strips of birch. Lem wondered and admired as the strong, firm fingers twisted and knotted, making all close and tight, and at last broke out with, —

"I say, mister, was you brought up to roof-mending?"

"Not exactly," replied Mr. Stanton, with a smile; "but I have had to contrive many a strange roof for myself and others. What should you say to a roof made of a single leaf, large enough to shelter twelve men from a scorching sun? Or to one of snow; ay, to roof, walls, floor, all of snow, — making a warm, comfortable home too?"

"Are you the fellow they tell about that's hunted lions and tigers and wild beasts?" asked Lem, gazing with new interest at the gentleman.

"I am the man," said Mr. Stanton.

"And never got ate up?" questioned Lem, eagerly.

"I am here to answer for that, though I have been pretty near it once or twice. Should you like to hear some of my adventures some time?"

"Wouldn't I, though! I s'pose you couldn't tell a feller now?"

"Not now," said Mr. Stanton, "we have done the best we can for the roof, and I must go home; but I shall come over again this afternoon to see Dolly, and I will tell you the story of a tiger hunt then. But" — looking about him, — "this is not a very nice place to sit down and tell a story in, with all these bones, ashes, and bits of old iron lying about."

"I'll fix it up, fustrate," exclaimed Lem; "but now, I say, mister," and Lem hitched up his ragged pantaloons, scratched his head, and dug his bare toes into a patch of moss in an unwonted fit of shame.

"Well," said Mr. Stanton, kindly.

"I didn't take little Shiny-hair's cup, now, I didn't; and I wish you wouldn't think it."

"I do not think it, Lem. The cup is found, and I do not believe you took it."

"Don't you, now?" said Lem, looking up; "well, I thought may be you didn't when you gi' me the money for the straw."

"I am glad to know that I may trust you, Lem," said Mr. Stanton.

Mr. Bradford, Mrs. Stanton, and the Porters had long since gone away, leaving Mr. Stanton to finish the roof. He walked slowly homeward, wondering if he had that morning really gained any hold on these wretched children;

or if, as so many others had proved, his pains had all been labor thrown away. When he reached the fireplace, he found that the rest of the party had gone home; for the mending of the roof had been a good two hours' work, and it was now nearly Mrs. Porter's early dinner hour.

When Mr. Bradford left Lem's hovel, and joined his wife and children, he found his little girls very eager for news of Dolly. He told them of all that had been done, and then said, —

"Bessie, I have a pleasant surprise for you. Can you guess what it may be?"

"I know what I would *like* it to be, papa, but I suppose it couldn't; and mamma said it was not best to wish for things that cannot be."

"Well," said Mr. Bradford, "suppose you let me hear what you would like it to be."

"Papa, I would like it to be my cup; but if it was, I would be *too* surprised and *too* glad for any thing, and I try not to think too much about it."

Mr. Bradford put his hand into his pocket,

and, pulling out the beloved cup, held it before the delighted eyes of his little daughter. She gave a glad cry, and the next moment both small hands were holding fast the recovered treasure, and clasping it to her breast. She even kissed it in her joy and thankfulness. Then papa was asked when and how he had found it, and told the whole story. Maggie and Bessie were very glad to hear that it was probably the pedler who had taken the cup; for since they had been trying to act and feel kindly towards Lem and Dolly, they were anxious to believe as much good and as little ill of them as possible.

"For you see, papa," said Maggie, "you see the pedler is quite a stranger to us, and we know Lem and Dolly a little. It's a pretty poor kind of a way to be acquainted, to be sure; but then we are pretty interested about them, and we like to think they did not do this one bad thing. And I think it would be rather astonishing if Dolly was not mad when Lem was shut up, and she knew he had not taken

Bessie's cup. I would have been, if some one had shut up Fred or Harry, and I'm afraid I would have wanted to return them a little evil; so now it is a little easier to forgive her about our gardens."

"And she said she was sorry about the gardens," said Bessie; "maybe it was her sorriness that made her tell where my cup was. Oh, my dear, dear cup! I am so glad it has come back."

And now the cup must have a good washing in the spring; after which, Bessie took a long drink from it. Not that she was in the least thirsty, but it was such a pleasure to drink once more from the beloved cup, and she thought no water had ever tasted so delicious. Then each one of her friends was obliged to take a drink, and to say how very nice it was; and for the rest of the day, she was every five minutes asking some one if they were not thirsty, and if she could persuade them to say yes, she would run and fill the cup. So much water did she and Maggie find it necessary to drink, and so much did they persuade, and even bribe, Frankie to take, that mamma was obliged to put a stop to the fun lest they should make themselves sick.

When Mr. Stanton and Mr. Bradford went up to the hut that afternoon, they found that Lem had been as good as his word. All the old bones and feathers, bits of rusty iron, half-burnt sticks, and ashes, had been picked up, and put out of sight. Lem had even made a poor broom out of some dry birch twigs and a stick, and with this he had tried to sweep off the broad slab of rock on which the house stood. It was not half done, to be sure; Lem was not used to sweeping, or to making things tidy; but he thought he had made the place very fine for his new friends, and they did not fail to praise and admire. Moreover, Lem had washed his face, for the first time perhaps in many weeks or months; and, although he had left his cheeks all streaked and channelled, it was at least an attempt at something better, and, so far, even this was promising.

Dolly was awake, but quite wild, and talked in a rambling way of silver cups and angels, of gardens and music, of the Ice Glen and the dark, dark night. Her fever was very high, and her poor head rolled from side to side; but, in spite of her restlessness, she could not move hand or foot, for the terrible pains which racked her and made her cry out on the slightest motion.

"She's awful sick, aint she?" said Lem, as he stood beside the two gentlemen, and saw with what grave faces they watched his sister.

"She is very sick, Lem," said Mr. Bradford; "too sick to be left here alone with you. I must go and see if I can find some one to come and take care of her to-night;" and, after saying a few words in French to his brother-in-law, Mr. Bradford walked away.

Mr. Stanton stayed behind. He had brought with him the upper half of an old window-sash which he had begged from Mr. Porter, a hammer, and some large nails; and he now told Lem they must go to work again, and he would tell the promised story as they worked. The sash was too large for the square hole in the side of the house which served for a window; but Mr. Stanton made it answer for the time, hanging it by strips of leather, nailed at one end to the sash, at the other to the boards above the window. This now served the purpose, since it could be raised or let down as might be needed. Then the crazy door was taken down, and hung anew on its two hinges; and, as the old latch was quite worn out and useless, Mr. Stanton fashioned a wooden button by which it might be fastened.

Meanwhile he told in low tones, that Dolly might not be disturbed, the story of a famous tiger hunt. Lem listened eagerly, — listened with ears, eyes, and mouth, if such a thing could be; for the two latter were so wide open that he seemed to be drinking in the tale by these as well as by the proper channel. But Mr. Stanton soon found he was not to be depended upon for work. Accustomed to an idle, lazy life, Lem could not fix his attention and employ his hands at the same time. If Mr. Stanton reminded him of his work, he would hammer or cut away for one moment; the next his hands would be clasping his knees in an ecstasy of delight and wonder at the strange but true tale he was listening to.

The gentleman let it pass, however. Lem's help was not of much account at the best; and his object just now was to gain a hold on the boy, and interest him. Teaching, advice, or reproof might come by and by, when he had made Lem feel he meant to be a friend to him.

Nevertheless, Lem had not the least idea that he had not done his own share of the work; and when the door and make-shift window were both in their places he exclaimed,—

"We did fix it up fustrate; didn't we mister?"

"I am glad you like it," said Mr. Stanton, looking about him. "What have you there, Lem?" and he pointed to four small rustic boxes standing at the side of the hut. They were made of twigs and bits of wood curiously woven together, and were filled with earth. Two of these held nothing else, in each of the others grew two scraggy little plants.

"Oh, them!" said Lem, "them's nothing but Doll's pots. She made 'em at odd times, always had a knack that way; and them things growin' in 'em is marygools, I guess. She picked up a paper with some seeds in it, on the road one day, and nothin' would serve her but to plant 'em. So she made the pots for 'em and stuck 'em in, but none of 'em come to nothin', only them two. I tell her there's lots of better lookin' things in the woods, to be had for the pickin'; but somehow she sets a heap by them old things, and waters 'em every day.

"Then you must take care of them for her, while she is sick; won't you?" said Mr. Stanton.

"S'pose so," said Lem; "but they'll never be no good."

XIII.

A RIDE ON THE SHEAVES.

MR. BRADFORD had gone in search of Mr. Porter; but when he reached the Lake House, he did not find him there; for this was harvest time, and the old man, still strong and hearty, was out in the fields, helping his sons and hired men to mow and carry in the grain. The whole flock of little ones, boys and girls, were out in the harvest fields too, and there went papa.

What a pretty, joyous sight it was! At the farther side of the fields, were the reapers, cutting with long, regular sweeps the yellow grain; while, nearer at hand, were others binding it in sheaves. Among these were Harry, Fred, and Hafed.

Upon an overturned sheaf, sat mammy, her

baby on her knee, the little one crowing and laughing, and shaking her dimpled hands, each of which grasped half a dozen ears of wheat, a new and wonderful plaything to baby's eyes, as they bobbed their heads up and down with the motion.

Near by, where the wheat still lay as it had been cut, in long even rows, was Frankie, in busy mischief as usual, snatching up whole handfuls of it, and tossing it above his head with shouts of glee. Mr. Porter would not have him stopped; no one minded a little more trouble, provided the children had their fun, he said. The old man himself stood by the side of the great ox cart, which was filled with golden sheaves; and on the top of these Maggie and Bessie sat in state, their hands and round straw hats filled with bright, red poppies. John Porter was about to give them a ride up to the great barn where the wheat was to be stored.

Mr. Bradford stood for a moment looking at it all, then walked up to Mr. Porter.

"Mr. Porter," he said, "can you tell me where I can find some one who will go and nurse that poor girl? She is too ill to be left with no one but her brother to take care of her."

Mr. Porter shook his head.

"I don't know of a soul that would be willing to go. 'Taint a place where one would care to pass the night, with the chance, too, of Owen coming home."

"If good pay could induce any one to do it, that shall not be wanting," said Mr. Bradford. "Is there no one in the village who would do it for that?"

"Well, I do know of a poor woman who might be glad to earn a little that way," said Mr. Porter; "but we could not get at her to-night. It is too late now to go down the mountain, with the roads washed as they were by the rain of night before last. There's no moon, and it would not be safe coming back; but I'll send for her in the morning, if you say so."

"I do say so," replied Mr. Bradford; "but what are we to do for to-night?"

Maggie and Bessie heard no more; for just then John Porter gave the word to his oxen, and they started off, leaving papa and Mr. Porter still talking.

What a pleasant ride that was: out of the field where the bars had been let down; past other fields ready, or nearly ready, for the harvesting; pale green oats, and golden wheat, the white, sweet-scented buckwheat, and the tall Indian corn; then through the orchard where a flock of sheep were feeding, past the locust grove, and then into the farmyard; stopping at last between the open doors of the great barn!

But, in spite of it all, our little girls were rather thoughtful as they jogged slowly on.

"Maggie," said Bessie, presently, "won't it be dreadful if papa can't get any one to take care of poor sick Dolly to-night?"

"Yes," said Maggie: "I wonder what she will do."

"If I was big, and mamma would let me, I'd go myself," said Bessie.

"Would you?" said Maggie; "well, I am afraid I wouldn't: so it's better that I am not big, 'cause then I needn't have a troubled conscience for not doing it."

They were both silent for a moment or two. John Porter was walking at his oxen's heads, out of hearing, if the children lowered their voices.

"Bessie," said Maggie, in a whisper, "John Porter might do it, mightn't he? He is big and strong enough."

"Yes," answered Bessie, "and he heard what papa said too; but he didn't say he'd go. Perhaps it didn't come into his head. Shall we try to put it there, Maggie?"

"Yes: maybe you can coax him to do it."

"I'll try, and see if I can make him compassioned of poor Dolly. John," she said, in a louder tone, "you are very glad you are well and strong; are you not?"

"Surely," said John.

"And you wouldn't like to be sick at all, would you, John?"

"Not one bit," said John. "I'd scarce know myself, for I never was sick in my life, that I remember."

"Then I s'pose you feel very thankful for it, and as if you'd like to help make sick people as well as you are; don't you?" said Bessie.

"Guess I wouldn't make much hand at that," answered John.

"But you are big and strong, John."

"Yes, I'm big and strong enough; but it takes more than that to make a good nurse. If it came in my way to do a good turn for a sick body, and there was no one else to do it, why I'd lend a hand; but I don't know as they'd thank me for it."

"Oh yes they would, John," said Maggie, eagerly; "if I was sick and had no one to take care of me, and you came to do it, I'd thank you ever so much."

"Well, I'll do it when you come to that

pass," said John, without the least idea what the little girls were driving at.

"He don't seem to understand yet," whispered Maggie to her sister; "try him with the 'Golden Rule.'"

"John," said Bessie, "are you not very fond of doing as you would be done by?"

"As fond as most folks, I guess," said John. "'Gee, there! gee, Whitefoot!'"

Bessie waited till they had passed through the gate of the orchard, then began again.

"John, if there was a chance to do as you would be done by, and you did not think of it, would you like some one to tell you of it?"

John looked round at her and laughed.

"If there's any thing you want me to do for you, out with it. It's no good beating about the bush. You know I always like to do for you what I can."

"Yes: you are very good to us," said Bessie; "but it was not us: it was Dolly. Don't you think it would be doing as you would be done by to go and take care of her to-night?"

"Whew! that's it, is it?" said John. "Maybe it would be; but that *would* be a good thing to see me taking care of Dolly Owen;" and John laughed loud and long.

Bessie was displeased, and drew herself up with a little dignified air.

"I don't think he is coaxed a bit," she whispered; "he is very hard-hearted."

"No," said Maggie: "I don't believe he is the kind to be coaxed."

"Then I'll have to be a little strict with him, and show him it's his duty," said Bessie, in the same tone.

"Yes, to let him see he ought to do it, whether he likes it or not," said Maggie; "maybe he's never been taught that."

"John," said Bessie, folding her little hands gravely in her lap, and trying to look sternly at the young man, "perhaps you don't know that if we know we ought to do a thing and don't do it, our Father is not very pleased with us."

"May be so," said John; "but I don't feel it's *my* duty to go and take care of Dolly."

"Whose duty is it, then?" asked Bessie.

"Not any one's that's likely to do it, I guess."

Bessie was in despair, but she thought she would try a little more severity.

"John," she said, "when you are poor and ragged, and sick and bad, I hope some one will have pity of you, and go take care of you."

"I hope so too; but I don't feel there's any call on me to go and look after that thieving beggar, nor for you to trouble yourselves about her, after all she's done to you," answered John.

"John," said Bessie, solemnly, "I'm afraid we don't think you quite so very nice as we did this morning; and I'm afraid you are one of those to whom our Lord will say, 'I was sick, and ye visited me not.'"

But John was only amused at her displeasure, and laughed aloud again.

Neither of the children spoke till they reached the barn, when John came to the side of the cart and lifted them down.

"Well, you are just two of the funniest,

forgivingest little things," he said, as he put Bessie on her feet.

Bessie deigned no answer; but with an air of great displeasure turned away, and stood at a little distance with Maggie, watching the men pitch the sheaves up into the loft.

"Are you going back with me?" asked John, when he was ready to start for the harvest-field again.

"No," Bessie answered, rather shortly.

"Why, you're not offended with me, are you?" said John, "and all along of that ragamuffin up there."

"We're displeased with you," said Bessie. "It's right to be displeased with people when you tell them what is right, and they don't do it; but if you're going to repent, we'll forgive you."

John answered with another "ha-ha."

"Well, no," he said; "I don't think I'm ready for repentance in that line yet. I hope I'll never do any thing worse than refusing to take care of a sick beggar."

"I hope so too," said Bessie, reprovingly. "That's quite worse enough," and she and Maggie walked out of the farmyard, and turned into the lane which led up to the house.

"Hallo!" John called out, mischievously; "if you feel so bad about Dolly, why don't you ask your father or uncle to go up and see after her?"

Neither of the little girls turned their heads, but walked straight on in the most dignified silence, followed by the sound of John's merriment.

"That's a little too much," said Maggie, when they were beyond hearing; "idea of papa or Uncle Ruthven staying all night in that dirty place!"

Bessie did not like the idea either, but her little head was puzzled. If she thought it right for John Porter to go, ought she not to think it right for her papa or uncle? She did not at all thank John for putting the thought into her head: it was fresh cause of offence against him; but now that it was there, she could not shut it out.

"Maggie," she said, "I wonder if we ought not to put it into papa's or Uncle Ruthven's mind?"

"Pooh! no," said Maggie; "they've sense enough to think it out for themselves if they ought to go: but I don't think John Porter is very sensible; do you?"

"I guess I won't say he's unsensible just now," said Bessie. "I'm 'fraid I feel most too mad."

"What difference does that make?" asked Maggie.

"'Cause mamma said, when I was angry it was better not to say unkind things about a person; and then when I was pleased with them again I would see that the unkind things were only in my own heart, and not quite true. She didn't say just those very words, but that was what she meant."

"I'm never, never going to be pleased with John Porter again," said Maggie, shaking her head very decidedly. "Oh! there's Mrs. Porter going to feed the chickens; let's go help her."

The chickens had been fed and had gone to roost, and the little girls had been with Dolly and Fanny to the pasture to see the cows milked, before they went back to the house, and met Uncle Ruthven just coming home. They ran up to him, and each taking a hand, asked for news of Dolly. It was not good, — worse, if any thing, than the last; and they looked rather sober as they walked with their uncle up the steps of the piazza, where all the rest of the family were gathered.

"Well," said Uncle Ruthven to papa, "have you had any success?"

"Not the least," said Mr. Bradford; and then he told what Mr. Porter had said.

"She must be looked after to-night," said Mr. Stanton. "Lem does not know what to do for her, and is frightened half out of his senses at the thought of being alone with her. It would be cruel to leave them."

"Yes," said Maggie, indignantly; "we were trying to make John Porter see it was his duty to go and take care of her, but he would not. He has not a bit of compassion."

"We said every thing we could, till we were quite despaired of him," put in Bessie; "but it was all of no use."

"What makes you think John Porter ought to go and take care of her?" asked Uncle Ruthven.

"Oh! 'cause he's such a big, strong fellow," said Maggie, "so we thought it was his duty; but he would not be put in mind of it."

"Well," said Uncle Ruthven, "there is another big, strong fellow whom you have put in mind of *his* duty. He had an inkling of it before, but I must say he was not very willing to see it."

"Ruthven!" exclaimed his wife, "you do not mean you are going to that dreadful place to pass the night!"

"I do not see that Maggie and Bessie have left me any choice," he answered, smiling, and sitting down on the steps beside her, " at least not if being a big, strong fellow makes it one's duty to go."

"Oh, Uncle Ruthven!" said Maggie, "we never meant you."

"Perhaps not, Maggie; but the shoe fits, so I think I must put it on."

"Is there no one we could find to do it if they were well paid?" said his wife, pleadingly.

"I expect to be well paid, love," he said in a low tone and with another smile. "I shall have all the reward I can ask."

Little Bessie was standing at Mrs. Stanton's knee, twisting one over another her aunt's soft, white fingers, and as her uncle spoke she looked up brightly.

"We know what he means, don't we, dear Aunt Bessie? He means the cup of cold water given in Jesus' name shall have its reward. I think Uncle Ruthven is taking up a jewel."

"Thank you, darling," said Aunt Bessie, with a quiver in her voice.

"For what, Aunt Bessie?"

But Aunt Bessie only smiled and kissed her, and Uncle Ruthven said, —

"I shall borrow the Colonel's camp chair with his permission, and take some candles and a book, so I shall do very well on this fine, still night."

"And I shall keep awake all night and think about you, Uncle Ruthven," said Maggie; "so if you feel lonely you can know my soul is over there with you."

So when tea was over, Uncle Ruthven with a lantern, the Colonel's camp-chair, and some other needful things for Dolly, went over to pass the night at the wretched hut.

The little girls stood beside Aunt Bessie and watched him as he walked away, and Bessie, taking Mrs. Stanton's hand in hers, laid her cheek upon it in her own caressing way, and said, —

"Aunt Bessie, I think we'll *all* have to try to bear Dolly's burden to night."

"It's too bad!" exclaimed Maggie; "it's an

awful burden to bear, it makes me feel homesick, and I want to cry about it, and I just will — there now!" and Maggie burst into tears.

Mamma came, and after a little petting carried them off to bed, for they were both tired. But on the way she had to stop in the kitchen to speak to Mrs. Porter, and there her little girls followed her and found John.

Now we know Maggie had said she "*never, never* meant to be pleased with John again;" but when he called to them, and said he had a treat for them the next day, she somehow found herself, she did not quite know how, talking away to him, and begging to know what it was, as if she had never been displeased with him in her life.

But after she was in bed and mamma had gone, she suddenly popped up her head and said, —

"Bessie, what do you think? I went and forgot I was mad with John Porter. Now, what shall I do about it?"

"I guess you'll have to stay unmad," said Bessie, sleepily.

"Yes, I s'pose I will," said Maggie; "and I believe I'm rather glad of it. I don't feel very nice when I keep displeased with people, and John is real good to us, if he wouldn't go stay with Dolly. Are you going to stay awake all night, and think about Uncle Ruthven?"

"I'd like to," said Bessie; "but I'm 'fraid I can't. I'm so tired and sleepy, my eyes won't stay open."

"Mine will," said Maggie. "I'm going to make them. I don't mean to sleep a single wink, but just think about Uncle Ruthven all the time. Isn't he kind and good, Bessie? John Porter is pretty good too: I wonder where he's going to take us to-morrow, and if mamma will let us go, — and s'pose — maybe — Uncle Ruthven in the — rocks — and I'm — not — going " —

"Maggie," said Uncle Ruthven, the next morning, "I rather think I missed the company of those constant thoughts you promised me last night, at least for part of the time."

Maggie climbed on her uncle's knee, put her

arms about his neck and her lips very close to his ear, and whispered,—

"*Please* don't tell any one, Uncle Ruthven; but I am afraid I did go to sleep for a few minutes last night. I didn't mean to, but I did"

XIV.

BLACKBERRYING.

"MAMMA, mamma, mamma!" cried Maggie and Bessie, dancing into the room with sparkling eyes and glowing cheeks.

"What is it, Sunbeams?" asked mamma.

"Oh! a blackberry party, mamma, — such a splendid blackberry party! — and we are all to go if you will let us. John is going to take us; and Dolly and Fanny are going, and Jane, too, if you would like to have her. Can we go, can we? Oh, say yes, mamma!"

"And please don't say I am too little, mamma," said Bessie. "John will take very good care of me, and carry me over all the hard places. And if we pick more berries than we want to eat for tea, Mrs. Porter is going to make them into blackberry jam for us to take home with us. So you see it will be very useful, as well as very pleasant, for us to go."

"Very well," said mamma, "that being the case, I think I must let you go."

Half an hour later the party started, armed with baskets and tin pails. Away they went, laughing and singing, by the lake road, and then down the side of the mountain to a spot where John said the blackberry bushes grew very thick. The way was pretty rough, and not only Bessie, but Maggie also, was glad of John's help now and then. Indeed, Bessie rode upon his shoulder for a great part of the way.

The blackberries were "thick as hops" when they came upon them, — some still green, some red or half ripe, others as black as ink; and these the children knew were what they must pick. The fingers of large and small were soon at work, but Maggie and Bessie did not find it quite as great fun as they expected.

"Ou, ou!" exclaimed Maggie, as she plunged

her hand into the first bush. "Why, there are horrid prickers on it!"

"And on mine too," cried Bessie. "They stick me like every thing. Oh, my finger is bleeding!"

"To be sure," said Fanny; "you must be careful: blackberry bushes are full of thorns."

Maggie and Bessie had not bargained for the thorns, and felt somehow as if they had been rather imposed upon; but they picked away more carefully. Now and then a berry found its way into a small mouth instead of into the pails, and very ripe and juicy it tasted.

By and by Bessie gave a little sigh and said,—

"Maggie, do you think it is so very nice?"

"I'm trying to think it is," said Maggie; "but they do scratch awfully, don't they? and the sun is pretty hot too. How many have you, Bessie?"

"I guess about five hundred,—maybe it's a thousand," said Bessie. "Can you count them?"

"Let's sit down there in the shade and do

it," said Maggie. "One, two, three, four,— there's seventeen, Bessie. That's a pretty good many."

" Is it most a thousand, Maggie ? "

" No," said Maggie, " I'm afraid it will take about fifty more to make a thousand. Here's Bob; we'll ask him," as Bob and Hafed came by with their baskets. " Bob, Bessie has seventeen berries; how many more will it take to make a thousand ? "

" Seventeen from a thousand," said Bob, " why it will take — nine hundred — and — and — eighty-three. You haven't the beginning of a thousand there yet."

" Have I enough to make a pot of jam ? " asked Bessie, wistfully, looking into her pail. " Your mother said she would make me a pot of my own if I brought enough berries."

" A small pot it would be," said Bob, laughing. " Take two to show the pattern, I guess," and he ran off.

Hafed lingered behind. He understood enough to know that Bessie was disturbed because she had so few berries; and suddenly emptying his basket, which was about a third full, into her pail, he said, —

"Me blackberry pick Missy Bess, all give."

"Oh! no, Hafed," said Bessie. "I thank you very much, but it wouldn't be fair to take your berries."

"Please, missy, make Hafed feel good," he answered, holding his basket behind him when Bessie would have poured the berries back. "Me much find; bring, too, some Missy Mag —" by which he meant he would bring some more to Maggie, — and he went after Bob.

"Oh! you're tired, are you?" said Jane, turning around to look what her young charges were doing, and seeing them on the rock. "Maybe you'd like a little lunch too; and here's some biscuits, and a couple of cookies your mother told me to bring lest you should be hungry. Then you can eat some of your berries; or, stay, I'll give you some of mine so you may keep all your own."

So the kind nurse opened the paper containing the biscuits, and spread it on the flat stone on which the children sat; next she pulled two broad mullein leaves, and put a handful of berries on each, and then having produced the drinking cup she always carried when the children went on an expedition, she asked John where she should find a stream, and one being near at hand as usual, the cup was soon filled and placed beside the other things.

"There," said Jane, "I don't believe Queen Victoria herself had a better set-out when she went blackberrying."

The children thought not; and the rest and unexpected little lunch made them both feel refreshed and bright again.

"Bessie," said Maggie, as they sat contentedly eating it, "do you not think foreigner boys are a great deal nicer than home-made boys?"

"What does foreigner mean?" asked Bessie.

"It means to come out of another country. Hafed is a foreigner, and that little French boy who was so polite to us on board the steamboat was a foreigner, and so is Carl."

Carl was Uncle Ruthven's Swedish servant.

"Are not Harry and Fred home-made boys, Maggie?"

"Yes; but, of course, I don't mean them: they're our brothers; but, of example, don't you think Hafed is a great deal nicer and politer than Bob?"

"Oh, yes! Bob laughed at me 'cause I had only a few berries; and Hafed did not laugh a bit, but gave me his."

"Midget and Bess," came in Fred's clear tones from a little distance, "come over here; here are lots of berries, lying on top of one another almost, ripe and sweet; and calling out, 'Come pick me!' They hang low, so we'll leave them for you, and it's nice and shady too."

"Fred is a nice home-made boy; is he not?" said Bessie, as they obeyed his call.

"Yes, and Harry too," said Maggie. "I did not mean to pass any remarks of them."

There were indeed lots of blackberries in the spot to which Fred had called them; and, screened from the rays of the sun, they picked them with comfort; besides which, many a large berry which they did not pick themselves found its way into their pails; so that, by the time Hafed came with his offering to Maggie, her own berries made quite a show, and she steadily refused to take his.

Then John said they must be moving homeward. They went by a different road from that by which they had come, stopping every now and then, where the berries were fine and thick, to add a few more to their store.

Seeing some which they thought particularly fine, the rest of the party climbed a steep rocky path to get them; while Maggie and Bessie, being tired, sat down to rest upon a fallen trunk. Suddenly a rustling beside them startled them; and, looking round, they saw a large pair of bright, soft eyes, gazing at them. A pair of ears were there also, a black nose too; in short, the whole of some animal's pretty head; and, before the little girls had time to call out or run away, a beautiful little fawn sprang out from the bushes and ran to them as if he was glad to see them. It had a red collar about its neck with some letters on it; but the children had no need to look at them: they knew the pretty creature quite well. It belonged to the little cousins down at the homestead, and was a great pet, and now it came rubbing its head against them, and putting its hoof into their laps, as if it were very glad to see some familiar faces. It must have wandered from home, the children knew; and so John said, when he came a moment later.

"I shall have to take the poor creature back," he said. "It would never do to take it up home, for Buffer would tear it to pieces; and, besides, they'll be worrying about it down there; so I'd better go at once. You can find your way home from here, Fan; take that right-hand path, and it will bring you out just below Owen's shanty"

The fawn seemed quite unwilling to leave the children; indeed it would not go at all, till John tied a string to its collar, and drew it after him. As it was found out afterwards, it had been lost since the day before; and the homestead children were in great distress, and had hunted for it in vain.

The path pointed out by John brought them, as he said it would, very near Owen's hut, and, looking towards it, they saw Mr. Stanton and his wife and Mrs. Bradford standing in front of it.

While Mr. Bradford had gone to the village to send the doctor, and try to find a nurse for Dolly, the two ladies had come with Mr. Stanton to see the sick child.

She was quieter than she had been through the night, but was, if any thing, more ill. She moaned incessantly, and Lem said, was all the time begging for something, he could not make out what.

Mrs. Stanton laid her soft, cool hand on the girl's burning forehead. Dolly seemed to like the touch, and looking up into the lady's face, said something in a beseeching tone.

"Do you want any thing, Dolly?" asked Mrs. Stanton, bending lower.

"I want," muttered Dolly; "I want to — to be angel."

"Poor Dolly," said the lady in a gentle, pitying tone.

"What is it she wants?" asked Lem.

"She says she wants to be an angel."

"Want to be an angel," moaned Dolly again. "Somebody loves the angels — up in His place — not tired there — rest for the weary; that's tired folks — that's me. I'm so tired — want to be an angel."

"Dolly," said Mrs. Stanton, not knowing if the girl could understand her, yet hoping that she might even now speak a word in season, "Dolly, you may be an angel some day if you will come to Jesus. He wants you to come and love Him. He wants you to be a good girl so that He may take you to His heaven, where there will be no more pain or sorrow, where you will never be tired, where you will be an angel. Will you love Him, Dolly; will you be a good girl, and try to please Him?"

"Don't love *me*," said Dolly, who, with her eyes fixed on the lady's face, had grown quiet, and really seemed to understand what she was saying; "loves little gals, maybe, what sings: they has nice frocks, and I aint fit for His beautiful place."

"Jesus will make you clean and white, and fit for His heaven, if you ask Him, Dolly. He does love you. He is waiting for you to come to Him."

"Little gals said He loved me; but can't ask Him, He don't come here."

"Yes, He does, Dolly. He is here now. You cannot see Him; but He sees you, and is sorry for you. Shall we ask Him to make you fit for heaven?"

"Yes," said Dolly.

"Dear Jesus," said the lady, "we ask Thee to give this little girl a new, clean heart, and to make her fit to live with Thee"—

"To be an angel," put in Dolly, eagerly.

"Make her fit to be an angel, make her love to please Thee, and, when it is time, take her to the home where there shall be no more pain or trouble. Amen."

"No more pain — no more trouble," murmured Dolly, her mind wandering again; "want to be an angel — I'll give her the cup," she cried; "they say it kills folks to be too long in the Ice Glen, but I can't get out; they'll send Lem to jail, will they? I'll fix 'em with their fine gardens — want to — rest for the weary."

Then her eyes closed, but presently opened again; and, looking from one to another of the kind faces above her, she said, —

"I say, did He see me give up the cup?"

"Yes," said Mrs. Stanton. "He sees all we do."

"And did He like me a little 'cause I did it?"

"Jesus was glad when He saw you give up the cup, Dolly, because it was not yours, and it was right for you to tell where it was. He is always glad when we do right, or when we are sorry for doing wrong."

" Can I speak to Him ? "

" Yes: He is always ready and willing to listen to you, my poor child."

" Guess I'll tell Him," muttered Dolly; and, trying to put her hands together as she had seen Mrs. Stanton do, she said, " Jesus, I'm true sorry I sp'iled them gardens, and I want to be a angel, if you *could* please to let me."

It was the first prayer that ever passed Dolly's lips; she did not even know it was a prayer; she only knew she was speaking to Jesus, the great friend of whom little Bessie and this kind lady had told her.

Then the poor child turned her face around and fell into one of her short, troubled slumbers; while Mr. and Mrs. Stanton and Mrs. Bradford went outside, followed by Lem.

The two ladies and the gentleman sat down upon the rocks, while Lem took his place in front of them, hugging up his knees, and star ing from one to another with half-frightened, half-sorrowful, looks. They were all silent for a little time, then Lem suddenly said, —

"Mister, when folks goes to be angels they mostly dies, don't they?"

"Always, Lem," said Mr. Stanton, gently. "Angels are happy spirits whom God has taken from all the pain and trouble of this world to live with Him in that happy home where sorrow and death never come."

"Is Doll going to die?" asked the boy.

"I cannot tell: that will be as God sees best. Dolly is very sick; but we will do for her all we can, and we will ask Him to make her His own little child, so that if she dies she may be fit to live with Him, and if she lives, she may be ready to serve Him and love Him on earth."

"I'll tell you, mister," broke forth Lem, after another moment or two of silence, "I was awful sorry when I heard what Doll did to them gardens after the little gals begged me out; but you see she didn't know it, and she thought I was took to jail. I guess she's sorry too. Wasn't you awful mad about it?"

"I did feel pretty angry, Lem; but we won't talk any more about that. I do not think either you or Dolly will trouble our little girls again; will you?"

"I shan't," said Lem, "and if Doll gets well and does, I'll fix her: that's all."

Lem scarcely spoke without using some very bad word, such as is not best for me to write or you to read; and Mr. Stanton was waiting his time to speak to him about this. It came now.

"But maybe she'll die," continued Lem. "Anyhow, you and your folks has been real good to me and Doll: what for I don't know, for we did plague you awful. I don't s'pose I'll ever get the chance to do you a good turn; but, if I do, you see if I don't."

"Lem," said Mr. Stanton, "you might do me a good turn now if you choose."

"Can I, though?" said Lem; "well, I will fast enough; for you're a fustrate fellow, and you tell fustrate tiger and bear stories. S'pose you don't know another, do you?"

"Plenty more," said Mr. Stanton; "what I want you to do for me, is not to use bad words."

"Never had no schoolin'," said Lem, a little sulkily.

"Schooling will not help you in the way I mean," said Mr. Stanton; and then he explained to Lem what kind of words he did mean, telling him how wicked and useless they were, and how it distressed those who loved God to hear His holy name taken in vain Lem said he would do so no more; but the habit was so strong upon him, that, even as he promised, he used more than one profane word to make the promise strong.

But now a cry from Dolly told that she was awake and suffering, and the two ladies went in, and found her quite wild again.

"I want to be a angel," she said; "there's no pain, no tired, there — where's the singin' — I like it," and so she wandered on, calling upon the little girls and begging them to sing. In vain did Mrs. Bradford and Mrs. Stanton sing for her the two hymns which had taken her fancy, she only looked about more wildly for Maggie and Bessie, crying that she wanted "little one and t'other one," to sing for her. She grew worse and worse, till at last even the presence of the two ladies seemed to make her more wild; and they went out, leaving Lem to do the best he could with her. Mrs. Bradford was just saying she did not know what to do, since the children were from home, when the blackberry party appeared at the turn in the wood-path.

"Here are the children, heaven-sent, I believe," said their mother, and she beckoned to her little girls.

They came running towards her, eager to show their berries, and to ask for news of Dolly. Mamma told them how ill she was, calling for them; and asked if they would go and sing for her.

Bessie said yes, at once; but timid Maggie looked half doubtfully at the dark, ugly, little house, and had a short struggle with herself before she could make up her mind to venture in. And after they were inside, she held Bessie tightly by the hand, and for a moment or two could scarcely find voice to sing.

Dolly's wild eyes turned towards them, and softened a little with pleasure at the sight; and her loud, hoarse cries ceased. It was evident she knew them.

"Sing, 'I want to be an angel,' my darlings," said mamma.

It was strange to see how the sweet sounds now soothed the sick child, though they had failed when tried by Mrs. Bradford and Mrs. Stanton. A love for music was, beside her affection for Lem, the one soft spot in poor Dolly's sinful, hardened heart; but the practised voices of the two ladies had not half the charm for her of the simple, childish tones which had first sung to her the hymn which had taken such hold upon her fancy, or rather on her heart. They sang it again and again, varying from that only to "Rest for the weary," for no other hymns seemed to satisfy the sick girl. She grew calm and quiet, and at last even appeared to forget her pain as she lay listening.

Once, when they paused, she beckoned to Bessie, and said, "Do you sometimes speak to Him?"

"To whom?" asked Bessie.

"To Him what has the angels, and is glad if we're good, — Jesus."

"Oh, yes!" said Bessie; "we speak to Him very often: when we say our prayers, that is speaking to Jesus; and He always listens too."

"Then you speak to Him for me, will you? You knows Him better than I do: I don't know Him much, only what you and the lady telled me, and what the song says."

"What shall we tell Him?" asked Bessie.

"Tell Him I'm so tired this long while, and the pain aches so, and if He *could* just let me be a angel, I'd never do so no more; and I'm sorry I plagued you, and I'll do just what He bids me. I'm sorry I broke Miss Porter's plate too."

"Yes, we'll tell Him," said Bessie gently; "but, Dolly, Jesus would like you to tell Him yourself too."

"I done it, and I'll do it some more," said Dolly, feebly; "make some more singin'."

Maggie and Bessie sang again, and before long poor Dolly's eyes closed, and she lay quietly sleeping; while our little girls, having left some of their berries for Lem to give her when she woke, went home with their mother and other friends.

XV.

A FRIEND IN NEED.

THREE weeks had passed away, and still Dolly lay very ill. The terrible rheumatic pains were better, it is true, and she could now be moved without causing her so much agony; but she had a racking cough and much fever, and showed, in many other ways, how very sick she was. Lem said she had had a cough for a good while before that night spent in the Ice Glen, and that she had always been complaining of feeling tired. The doctor from the village shook his head when he was questioned about her, and so did Mr. Stanton and old Mrs. Porter. She had not wanted for such care as could be given her in her wretched home. Mr. Bradford had found a woman who, in consideration of being well paid, was willing to come and take care of her, and kind Mrs. Porter provided her with such food as she could take. Maggie and Bessie, and some of the ladies from the Lake House, came up to see her every day when the weather permitted, and would sing to her, and tell her of Jesus and His love.

It was strange to see how readily she listened, how eagerly she drank it all in, especially when Bessie talked to her. Perhaps the simple, earnest words of this little teacher were easier to be understood by her poor, untaught mind, than those of others who were older and wiser. Or it might be that she felt Bessie had been her first friend, — the first one to extend to her the hand of forgiveness and kindness, — or perhaps it was both of these things. However it was, she was always glad to see the little girls and have them tell her of that Friend above who was so full of pity, love, and forgiveness.

Dolly had heard of God before, but not as the kind, loving Father, — the merciful, gracious

Saviour, — who stands ready to receive all who will turn to Him, who comes after us when we go from Him, and who had now put out His pitying hand to draw to Himself this poor little stricken lamb who had wandered so far from his fold. She had heard His holy name taken in vain every day of her miserable little life; she had never until now heard it spoken in love and reverence; and the only idea she had had of Him, had been as some great but terrible being who some day might find her out, and punish her for the naughty things she had done. But the dread of this uncertain punishment had not checked her in her wicked ways; and so she had gone on, till the God she did not love and scarcely feared, had laid his hand upon her, and then sent these little messengers to bring to her the glad tidings of peace and pardon.

Day by day she grew more gentle, more humble, more quiet, more unlike the Dolly of old, on whom kindness and harshness had both been thrown away. Poor child, perhaps it was that she had had so much of the latter, that she had not known how to believe in the former when it came to her. It was touching to see her penitence for past offences, and how anxious she now became to be forgiven by those whom she had wronged. But her ideas of right and wrong were still very strange, and rather difficult to deal with.

One day Mrs. Porter came to see her and brought some nice broth, with which she fed her. As she was leaving, Dolly called her back, and told her to look in the corner beneath a heap of dried sticks and see what she would find. Willing to please the child, Mrs. Porter did so, and drew out a soiled but fine pocket-handkerchief.

"There," said Dolly, "I'm going to give you that for your plate that I broke. I'm right sorry I broke it. Jesus didn't like me much then, I guess."

Mrs. Porter was quite sure that Dolly had not come honestly by the handkerchief, and would not take it, which greatly distressed the child. Just at that moment, Mrs. Bradford came in, and Mrs. Porter told her the trouble.

"Dolly," said Mrs. Bradford, gently, "where did you get this handkerchief?"

"Off old Miss Mapes' currant-bush," said Dolly, promptly; adding, in an aggrieved tone, "I want her to have it 'stead of her plate, and she won't."

"Because it is not yours to give away."

"Then 'taint mine to keep," said Dolly; "and I guess Jesus don't want me to have it."

"He wants you to give it back to Mrs. Mapes, because that is the only right thing to do, Dolly."

"Old Miss Mapes is hateful," answered Dolly. "She chased me off the road when I didn't do nothin', and threw a hoe at me and cut my foot, and that's why I took it; I'd liever Miss Porter would have it. She's good."

"But if you want to be a good girl, and please Jesus, you must do what He wants you to, not what you had rather do yourself."

"Would He rather I'd give the handkercher back to Miss Mapes?"

"Yes," said Mrs. Bradford. "He was grieved when He saw you take it; and He will know you are truly sorry if you send it back to her."

"I'll do it, then," said Dolly; "you can take it to her: but don't you tell her I did it for her, 'cause I don't, — it's only for Him."

Poor child! it was perhaps as much as was to be expected from one so ignorant; and Mrs. Bradford, fearing to do her harm, said no more, trusting that even this blind striving after right was pleasing in the eyes of Him who has said, that little should be required of him to whom little has been given.

"Say 'Gentle Jesus,'" said Dolly, turning to Bessie, who had stood by while her mother was talking.

Next to the two hymns which had first taken her fancy, this seemed to be the one Dolly liked best; and now she often asked for it. Bessie repeated it. When she came to the two last lines of the second verse, —

> "In the kingdom of thy grace,
> Give a little child a place,"

Dolly said, "I'm going to say, 'Give a better child a place,' 'cause I'll be a better child now: true I will."

"With Jesus' help, Dolly," said Mrs. Bradford.

"He did help me," said Dolly. "He let her"—motioning towards Bessie—"come and tell me about Him."

The small, dirty hut, with the hard ground for its floor, its miserable roof, and chinks and crannies which let in the wind and damp, was no place for a sick child on these cool August nights; and now that Dolly could be moved without putting her to so much pain, it was thought best it should be done. The poor-house was many miles away, and now that Maggie and Bessie had come to take such an interest in her, and she in them, Mr. Porter said it would be cruel to send her so far, and offered to have her put in the old tool-house. So, for two or three days, the four boys and

Starr busied themselves in repairing it for her, papa and Uncle Ruthven furnishing what they needed to make it comfortable. A few planks and nails, a little whitewash and paint, a sash-window, and some willing hands, soon made it secure against wind and rain. Then Mrs. Porter had it cleaned, and a cot-bed, a pine-table, and two chairs were put in it. Plain and bare enough it was, to be sure, but a wonderful contrast to Dolly's former home; and the children thought with great pleasure of seeing her brought there. This was to be done in a few days, but Dolly was not to be told of it until the time came.

As Maggie and Bessie were on their way home with their mother, they met Uncle Ruthven and Aunt Bessie, the Colonel and Mrs. Rush, all going for a walk, and were invited to join them. Mamma agreed, if Bessie were not too tired, but the little girl declared she was not; and Uncle Ruthven promised to take her on his shoulder if she gave out before they reached home. Many a ride had the little "princess" taken on this kind, strong shoulder during their mountain rambles, and she now often wondered that she could ever have had "objections" to this dear, loving uncle who was always so ready to help and please her. So they all turned back together, and, passing by the end of the lake, struck into the road which led down the mountain. They strolled slowly down this for some little distance, and then Mrs. Bradford, and Colonel and Mrs. Rush, sat down to rest before they began their homeward walk; while Mr. and Mrs. Stanton and the two little girls wandered about, gathering wild flowers and mosses. Blue gentians, golden-rod, Michaelmas daisies, and the pretty, red partridge-berry grew all about, and the children soon had their hands full.

Suddenly, Maggie spied a cluster of bright scarlet maple leaves, the first of the season. The gravelly side of the mountain sloped away here for a few feet, then fell sheer down in a tremendous precipice to the valley beneath; and a foot or so below the edge grew this beautiful, tantalizing bunch of leaves. It was quite beyond Maggie's reach, for she had been forbidden to go near that side of the road, where a slip, or false step, might have sent her down, down a thousand feet.

"O Aunt Bessie!" she cried, "look what a lovely bunch of red leaves. It is just what you said you wanted for that c'llection you are making. I wonder if Uncle Ruthven could not reach it for you."

Aunt Bessie turned and looked.

"I can reach it for myself," she said. "Uncle Ruthven is upon the rocks, after those climbing-ferns. I will stand here and hook it up with this crooked stick."

"Take care, Bessie, take care!" called her brother, the Colonel; "that is loose gravel there; if it slips with you, you are lost;" and, 'Come back, Bessie, come back!" called her husband from above, seeing the danger more plainly than any of the others.

It was too late. She looked up, kissed her

hand gayly to her husband, and turned to obey. But her foot was already upon the treacherous gravel, and she slipped a little, recovered herself; then, startled, tried too suddenly to spring upon firmer ground, and slipped again. The gravel gave way more and more beneath her weight. She went sliding, sliding down, and, in an instant, had disappeared from the sight of the terrified group above.

"Ruthven! O Ruthven!" was the wild cry that rang out on the still summer air, followed by a shriek of terror from the two little girls, and a groan from the Colonel's lips. Then a stillness like death itself, and the next moment Uncle Ruthven stood among them.

But — how very strange Maggie and Bessie thought it — he did not seem frightened at all. His face was very white, to be sure; but his voice was steady and quiet, only it did not sound like Uncle Ruthven's voice, but like that of some stranger, and as if it came from far, far away.

"She is holding by the bushes below," he said; and, as he spoke, he threw himself flat upon the ground, half on, half over, the edge of the precipice, and, reaching one arm, he succeeded in grasping, and but just grasping, the wrist of his wife.

For it was as he had said. As she slid downwards, Mrs. Stanton had clutched wildly at the bushes growing below, and had succeeded in laying hold of them. But the bushes were slender, and not deeply rooted in the loose gravelly soil, and though Mrs. Stanton was a small, slight woman, even her light weight was too much for them, and they were just giving way, when her husband's strong, firm grasp was upon her wrist. Yes, he had her fast, holding back the precious life; but for how long? and what was to be done next?

Mr. Stanton dared not rise upon his feet or even upon his knees, and so try to draw her up; he was a large, heavy man; the treacherous edge, which would not bear his wife's far lighter weight, would give way beneath his,

and send them both to a fearful death below
Even now loose pebbles and gravel were falling
down, and striking upon the sweet, upturned
face which looked to him for help. Had her
feet even been upon the slope, or the ledge
beneath it, he might have drawn her up; but
they were below it, hanging over that terrible
precipice.

In vain did the Colonel, kneeling beside his
brother-in-law, clasp his arms about his waist,
and so try to draw both him and his sister to
a place of safety; the ground only broke away
more as the added strain came upon Mr. Stanton's arm, and a fresh shower of gravel and
stone went rolling down upon the poor sufferer
below.

Then came her voice in feeble tones. "Ruthven, it is of no use, love; my clothes are caught
and I cannot free them. Let me go, my husband: it is only throwing away your life."

"Not while God gives life and power to this
hand. Courage, my darling, courage. Go,
some of you, for help, ropes and men," he said,

turning his haggard face towards the others, and still speaking in that strange tone, so unlike his own.

In an instant, Mrs. Bradford was far up the road on her way to the house. To her little girls she seemed scarcely to touch the ground; to herself, it seemed as though leaden weights were upon her feet, and that she made no way at all. Just as she reached the lower end of the lake, she met her husband coming down to join them. Scarcely pausing, she spoke half a dozen words which sent him in haste on his way; then herself sped on towards the house.

Meanwhile, how long the moments seemed to the agonized group below. There was nothing more to be done till help came. Could Mr. Stanton hold on, could that cruel gravel bear them both, till that should be? God, in whom alone they trusted, only knew.

Mrs. Rush sat white and sick upon the bank, the little girls clinging to her and crying bitterly, but quietly. No sound broke that terrible stillness, except Uncle Ruthven's voice as he now and then spoke a few words of hope and encouragement to his wife, till a bird lighted a little way off, and broke into a joyous song. Maggie could not bear it: it seemed a mockery of their grief and agony; and, although at another time she would have been shocked at herself for doing such a thing, she now chased it away.

"Oh! why don't help come to us?" she sobbed out. "Why don't God send us help?"

Bessie raised her head from Mrs. Rush's lap, where she had hidden her face.

"Maybe we did not ask Him quite right," she said. "Aunt May, say a prayer for Aunt Bessie and for us all."

Mrs. Rush tried to speak, but could not. One ceaseless, agonized prayer had been going up from her heart; but she could not put it into words, and only shook her head. Bessie looked at her for a moment, and then, as if she under stood, said,—

"Shall I say it, Aunt May?"

Mrs. Rush nodded assent; and, kneeling at her side, Bessie clasped her little hands, and looking up to heaven, said, —

"Dear Father in heaven, we are so very troubled, we don't any of us know quite what to say; but you know what we want, even if we can't find the words, and our heart-prayers do just as well for you. Please send dear Aunt Bessie some help very quick. Have pity on her, and make her know our Father don't forget her. Amen."

It was said with many a gasp and sob of terror and distress; and, when it was finished, the little one hid her face in Mrs. Rush's lap again.

But she was right. The all-merciful Father had heard their earnest "heart-prayers," which could not be put into words; and help, such as they did not look for, was at hand.

None saw the figure bounding down the mountain side with such headlong speed — now swinging itself down some steep ascent by the branches of a tree, now springing from rock to rock like a wild goat — till it stood among them, breathless and eager.

The Colonel had risen to his feet, and, going a few steps up the bank where the ground was firmer, grasped the trunk of a tree for support, and looked over the edge at his poor sister. God had been merciful to her, and now sense and feeling had left her, and she hung unconscious in her husband's hand. Colonel Rush saw now what he had not known before, — a narrow ledge of rock, scarce six inches wide, jutted beyond the slope of gravel, and, on this, his sister's form partly rested. Well that it was so, or not even her husband's tremendous strength could have supported the strain so long. The Colonel eyed this ledge eagerly. It must have been on this that his brother-in-law relied, when he called for men and ropes. Could some one but reach it, and be held from above, they might fasten a rope about his sister's waist, and so she be drawn safely up. Could Ruthven hold on till then?

The Colonel looked around him, for a moment, with a wild thought of trying to reach it himself; the next he put it away as worse than folly. There was no rope, nothing to hold him or his sister; and if there had been, who was there to support and guide it? No one but a weak woman and two little children. He himself was a tall man, of no light weight, and with a lame foot: the attempt was sure to bring destruction upon himself, his sister, and her husband.

As he turned away, with another silent appeal for help, Lem stood before him.

"I seen it up there," he said, hurriedly, "and thought I'd never git here. I say, mister,"— to Mr. Stanton,—"if I only had a rope, or a bit of something to fasten about me, I know I could get down there, and put it about her, so you could histe her up."

The quick eye of the boy, used to all manner of make-shifts and hair-breadth escapes, had taken it all in, and saw a way of safety, if the means were but at hand. He looked

around, and spied a light shawl lying un
heeded upon the ground. He snatched it up,
tried its strength, and shook his head.

"'Twon't do," he said, "'taint long enough
so; and, if we split it, 'twon't be strong
enough."

The children and Mrs. Rush had risen, and
were listening; and now a quick thought
darted into Maggie's mind.

"Uncle Horace," she said, springing eagerly
forward, and pointing to the broad plaid ribbon about her sister's waist, "there's my
sash and Bessie's. Wouldn't they be of any
use?"

"Thank God! the very thing!" exclaimed
the Colonel; and, in an instant, the broad, stout
ribbons were untied from the children's waists,
and strongly knotted together.

"Can you hold the boy, Horace?" asked
Mrs. Rush.

"With God's help, and what you can give
me, I trust so," he answered.

"You must keep far enough from the edge

not to slide over yourselves, you see," said Lem, coolly, as he and the Colonel drew strongly upon the knot.

The Colonel measured the ribbon with his eye. Tied around Lem's waist, it would scarcely give the length they needed, and it was not safe to fasten it to any of the boy's ragged, worn-out clothes. He snatched up the shawl, twisted and wound it about Lem's waist, fastening it securely, then drew the ribbon through it. As he did so, Bessie cried out, —

"Papa! here's dear papa! That is help."

No one could bring such help as papa, Bessie thought; and there he came, running down the hill, and stood among them. A few words made him understand what they were about; and, as Lem was now ready, he, with the Colonel, took fast hold of the long ribbon.

Slowly and carefully, with the Colonel's cane in his hand, the boy stepped over the edge, — not just above Mrs. Stanton, but at the spot where the Colonel had looked over at her, —

down, step by step, till he had disappeared from the sight of all but Mr. Stanton, who, lying over the edge, watched him, God only knows, with what sickening hope; the loose soil crumbled and slid beneath him; but, light and sinewy as he was, his bare feet, trained to all kinds of mountain climbing, took hold where those of a heavier person, with shoes upon them, must have faltered and slipped past all recovery. He had reached the ledge, and now, step by step, slowly neared the lady. Sure-footed as a goat, steady of head and nerve, reckless of danger, yet with sense enough to remember the Colonel's charge not to look below him, he reached her side, freed her clothes from the clinging bushes; then, with a care and steadiness which Mr. Stanton, spite of his agonizing anxiety, wondered to see, unrolled the shawl from his own body, and fastened it about that of the senseless figure beside him; then gave the word to raise her.

Up, up, steadily, inch by inch, was the precious form drawn, till her husband's arm could grasp her waist, and she was lifted safe, — but oh! so white and still, — and laid upon the grassy bank; while Uncle Ruthven, almost as white, fell exhausted beside her. But he was on his knees and bending over her, by the time that Mr. Bradford and Colonel Rush had lowered the ribbon again; and Lem, flushed and triumphant, was drawn up unhurt. The boy was very proud, and perhaps justly so, of the feat he had performed, and would have broken out into some loud, exultant expressions, if Mr. Bradford had not checked him; and then, before a word was spoken, the gentlemen uncovered their heads, and Mr. Bradford spoke a few words of earnest, solemn thanksgiving for the wonderful mercy just shown them. Lem stared, openmouthed; and the instant he was allowed to speak, sprang forward to Mr. Stanton, —

"I told you I'd do you a good turn, if I got the way, mister; and I did, didn't I?"

"By God's mercy, yes," said Mr. Stanton.

"May he bless you for this, my brave boy. I will be a friend to you as long as I live."

Lem immediately turned half a dozen somersets, which, in spite of their admiration and gratitude, greatly disgusted Maggie and Bessie; for they did not see how he could have the heart to do such a thing while dear Aunt Bessie lay there, so white and still. They could scarcely believe Aunt May's assurance that she was not dead, but had only fainted, and were still filled with terror and distress.

And now, Uncle Ruthven lifted her in his arms, and they all set out on the way home; Lem keeping close to Mr. Stanton with his precious burden, as if he felt that he had some sort of a claim on her. But when they were about half way home, they met all the men and boys from the Lake House coming down the road with ropes, and Lem was taken with a sudden fit of shyness, and, turning about, rushed away without a word.

XVI.

LEM'S SORROW.

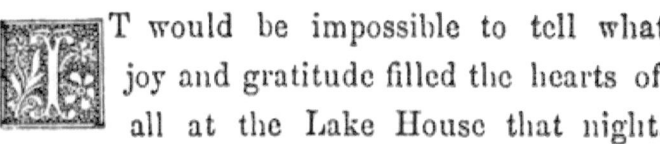T would be impossible to tell what joy and gratitude filled the hearts of all at the Lake House that night. It was true, indeed, that the dear one who had been snatched from such a fearful death was very ill from the fright and shock, weak and exhausted, and dreadfully nervous. Her arm, too, was badly hurt with the long-continued strain upon it, and her sweet face scratched and bruised with the falling stones and gravel; but the precious life had been spared, by God's great mercy, and they might hope, that, in a few days, she would be herself again.

The whole family had been sadly shaken by the terrible accident. Not only on that night, but for several succeeding ones, Maggie and

Bessie were constantly starting awake with cries of fear, and then they would sob and tremble so, that it was difficult to quiet them. Maggie would burst into tears for the merest trifle, — sometimes, even if she were spoken to suddenly, and then would cry and laugh by turns; and Bessie was often found in some corner, with her face hidden, sobbing as if her heart would break. "Just because I could not help it, mamma," she would say, when asked the reason; and she would shudder and quiver all over, at the least mention of that dreadful day. The shock had been too much for the tender young hearts, and it took them some time to recover from it.

It was necessary to keep the house very still, on account of Aunt Bessie, who was so very nervous that the least sound disturbed her; and roguish, noisy Frankie was, by Aunt Patty's earnest request, allowed to go to her house, where, for a few days, he lorded it over that humble servant of his to his heart's content. But there was no need to send the little girls away; they were only too quiet, and moped about the house in a way that was quite melancholy to see. The weather was damp and rainy, so they could not be much out of doors; and, although their friends did all they could to divert them with stories, reading aloud, and games, they did not seem able to shake off their sadness. The truth was, they could not forget Aunt Bessie's face, as they had seen it lying on Uncle Ruthven's shoulder, white and still; and it scarcely seemed possible to them that she could ever be well again.

But one day, grandmamma, coming out of Aunt Bessie's room, found the two little maidens sitting disconsolately on the stairs, looking wistfully at the door of the sick-room. She stepped back, spoke a few words to those within, and then, coming to the children, asked them if they would like to go and see the dear invalid. Bessie sprang eagerly forward, but Maggie, with the fear of seeing Aunt Bessie look as she had done on that dreadful day, hung back a little, till Bessie urged her forward.

They went in with hushed steps, for grandmamma said they must be very quiet, stay but a moment, and on no account must they speak of the accident. There lay Aunt Bessie on the pillows. Very white still was her face; but life and love looked out at them from the dear eyes: it was Aunt Bessie's own sweet smile which welcomed them, her own gentle voice which told them how glad she was to see them, her own warm kiss which met theirs.

"Aunt Bessie!" said her little namesake, and then she nestled her face on the pillows beside her, and said no more. But there was no need: there was a whole world of tenderness and joy in those two words, and Aunt Bessie felt it.

Maggie said nothing, but stood with swimming eyes, and rising color, gazing at her aunt, till Mrs. Stanton said,—

"Have you not a word for me, dear Maggie?"

Then Maggie gave a wistful kind of a smile,

and tried to speak, but broke down in a half-choked sob.

"Do not be worried about me, dearie," said Aunt Bessie; "I shall be quite well again in a few days."

Maggie did not answer, except by gently kissing the poor hurt hand, which lay upon the coverlet; but it was plainly to be seen that she was a good deal excited; and Uncle Ruthven, fearing one of her sudden bursts of crying, said the children had stayed long enough, and led them from the room.

Then Maggie's tears came forth, but they were happy tears, for she and Bessie were both satisfied about Aunt Bessie now; and she soon wiped them away, and from this time was her own bright, merry self.

And that afternoon there was a new subject of interest for them, for the weather cleared up warm and beautiful, and it was thought safe to bring Dolly to the better quarters provided for her. Mrs. Bradford and Mrs. Porter went to tell her what was to be done, and then came John Porter and one of his brothers to carry her over. They lifted her bed between them, and moved as carefully as possible, but it was a rough way, with many ups and downs, and spite of all their care Dolly suffered very much.

As they left the shanty, the sick child raised her head a little, and, looking towards the side where her flower-pots stood, cried out,—

"Oh! my posy boxes, bring 'em along, Lem."

Lem obeyed, and, taking up the two flower-pots which contained the scragly, sickly looking plants, trotted along beside Mrs. Bradford with one on each arm.

"She sets such a heap on the old things," he said to the lady as if in excuse. "I'm sure I don't know what for; but since she's been better, she's like crazed about 'em, and would have 'em brought in every day for her to see. I've watered 'em all along 'cause *he* told me to."

The *he* of whom Lem spoke was Mr. Stanton; and whatever he said and did had become right in the boy's eyes. Lem had improved a good deal during these three weeks, though the change was by no means so surprising in him as it was in Dolly. Dolly was trying in her own simple, ignorant way, to please that Heavenly Friend of whom she had so lately learned; while Lem, as yet, looked no higher than man's praise. Still it was much that such a hold had been gained upon the boy. He looked up to Mr. Stanton with a blind admiration and desire for his approval, which kept him from much mischief and wrong-doing. It was very strange, he thought, that this magnificent gentleman — whose appearance, tremendous strength, and wonderful adventures, made him a great hero in Lem's eyes — should trouble and interest himself so much about a poor, ragged boy, for whom every one had a hard word; and who, Lem knew very well, richly deserved all that could be said of him. To please Mr. Stanton had now become the aim of Lem's life, and with this purpose he was learning to give up many of his old bad ways. Mr. Stanton had even partly succeeded in curing him of his habit of using bad words every time he spoke. One day when he was telling the boy a story in which he was much interested, Lem suddenly broke out with some expression of delight, mingling with it a dreadful oath. Mr. Stanton immediately ceased his tale; and, when asked by Lem why he did so, told him that he could not talk to a boy who dared to take the name of his Maker in vain. Lem was disappointed, and angry too, but it did him good; and when, the next day, the gentleman offered to finish the interrupted story, he was very careful not to offend again. This happened more than once, and each time Lem became more unwilling to risk not only the loss of his story, but also the look of grave displeasure on his new friend's face. He also tried to keep the old place a little tidier, and, when he knew that any of the family from the Lake House were coming there, would wash his face and hands; and a comb having been brought by some of the ladies for Dolly's use, he would draw it a few times through his tangled locks. On the day before this, Mrs. Bradford had given him an old suit of Harry's, and he was now dressed in this, which, though too large for him, was at least clean and whole; and a proud boy was Lem as he walked by the lady's side.

Lem thought himself rather a hero, and not without reason, for the share he had had in saving young Mrs. Stanton's life; and was much inclined to talk of it to any one who would listen to him. He was still rather shy of the boys; but since the little girls had been so often to see Dolly, he had been quite friendly with them; and they were ready enough to allow him all the credit he deserved for the service he had rendered to their dear Aunt Bessie. Poor boy! praise and encouragement were so new to him, that it was perhaps no wonder he craved all that could fall to him.

On that memorable afternoon, he had been sitting on the rock in front of the hut, watching our friends as they sauntered down the road below him. He saw them stop, some sitting down to rest, while Mr. and Mrs. Stanton and the little girls wandered about in search of flowers.

He saw the lady fall, and was off in an instant, dashing over every thing which lay in his way, with a reckless, headlong speed, that soon brought him to the spot. Thanks to his wild, rambling life, Lem knew every foot of the mountain, and, even as he went, thought of what he might do, quite sure that he could keep his footing on that narrow ledge, if he could but once reach it. How well he had done, we know; and Lem knew right well himself, and meant that others should know it too. Too much puffed up in his own conceit, he certainly was; but we must remember how ignorant he was, and even this was better than that he should feel himself the miserable, degraded outcast of a few weeks since, whose "hand was against every man, and every man's hand against him."

He had not seen Mr. Stanton since the day of the accident; for, now that his wife was ill, the gentleman had not the time and attention to give to him and Dolly that he had before; but he knew that he was not forgotten, for more than one kind message had been sent to him.

"Think I could get a sight of my gentleman, to-day?" he asked of Mrs. Bradford.

"Of my brother?" said the lady. "Yes, I think so; he said he would see you when you came to the Lake House."

"That was a fustrate job I did for him — getting the lady up; now, warn't it? He said he'd never forget it."

"We shall none of us forget it," said Mrs. Bradford; "but, Lem, when one has done a great kindness to another person, it is better not to talk of it too much."

"No, I aint goin' to," said Lem, with a self-satisfied air. "I'll tell you if it hadn't been for me, the lady would have been gone afore those fellers got there with the ropes. He couldn't ha' held on much longer, and like enough they'd both gone down together."

Mrs. Bradford shuddered at the thought.

"Now, what do you s'pose he's goin' to do for me?" continued Lem. "Somethin' fustrate?"

"I think he is going to try to teach you to do right, and to put you in the way of earning an honest living, Lem. What would you like him to do for you?"

"Well," said Lem, "you give me these clothes, and now I'd just as lieve he'd give me one of his old hats and a red shirt; so I'd be decent-like; and then I'd like him to get me to be an engine driver on one of them railroads. If it wasn't for Dolly I'd like to be sent off on a ship to the place where the tigers and elephants is, so I could hunt 'em. But then she'd be lonesome after me; and if I was engine driver, I could come home every spell and see her. And I'm goin' to fix her a fustrate home, when I get a livin'. But I was thinkin' what will I do with her meantime. Do you think if *he* spoke a word for her, Porters would let her stay round their place? I guess she wouldn't plague 'em none now; and, when she gets well, she could do errands and such like for them."

Mrs. Bradford thought this a fitting time to tell Lem what he must know sooner or later.

"Dolly is going to a better home than any that you or we can give her, Lem," she said, gently. "She is going to that home which Jesus has made ready for her, — His own bright, glorious heaven, where she will never be tired or sick or hungry any more."

Lem stopped short in the path, and turned to the lady.

"She aint, I tell you," he said, fiercely. "You mean she's a goin' to be an angel, — what she's always talking about nowadays, — and she'll have to die for that, — *he* said so, — and she aint agoin' to. She's better now, I know; for she don't screech out with the pain like she used to."

"No," said Mrs. Bradford, standing still

beside him, as he looked down the path after Dolly and her bearers, "she does not suffer as she did; but she is more ill and grows weaker every day. She cannot live many days, Lem; and she knows that she is going to Jesus, and wanted that you should be told."

Lem set down the flower-pots, and dug his knuckles into his eyes.

"She shan't neither," he exclaimed. "I'm goin' to ask *him* to make her well. He can do it, I know; and, if he will, I won't ask him for nothin' else along of the good turn I done him, gettin' up the lady."

"My poor boy," said Mrs. Bradford, pityingly, "neither my brother, nor any other person can do more for Dolly than to make her comfortable for the few days she will be here. Her life is not in his hands, or in the doctor's, but in those of God, who sees best to take her to Himself."

Lem threw himself passionately upon the ground.

"'Taint fair," he sobbed. "She's all I've

got, and I always was good to her, now; ask her if I wasn't. I always gave her half what I got, and I saved her many a beatin'."

"Yes," said Mrs. Bradford, sitting down beside him, and laying her hand with a soothing touch upon his arm, "Dolly says you have been a good brother to her, and the only thing that makes her sorry to go is the fear that you may miss her."

"Like enough I'll miss her," said Lem, in a sullen kind of sorrow.

"But," said Mrs. Bradford, "you may see her again if you will live so that Jesus may some day take you to dwell with Him in His glorious home. Will you not try to do this, Lem?"

"Couldn't no way," replied Lem, sitting upright; "they say only good folks get to heaven, and don't you know they say I'm the worst boy here about? They used to say Doll was the worst girl too, and — don't you tell nobody I said it — she did do a heap of bad things, that's so! How's she goin' to get to heaven?"

"God says in His Word, 'believe on the

Lord Jesus Christ and thou shalt be saved.' Dolly does believe on her Saviour, and He will wash her soul from all its sin and fit it to live with Him. He has given her but little time to serve Him on earth since she has learned to love and trust Him; but she is doing all that she can: she is sorry for past sin, and whatever she thinks Jesus would like her to do, she tries to do."

"She's gettin' awful good, that's true," said Lem. "She made you take back old Miss Mapes' handkercher, and made me go and tell Miss Jones she was sorry for unhookin' her clothes-line and lettin' down the clothes in the dirt; and, oh! do you think, there's the biggest kind of a squash down in Todd's cornfield, and I was a goin' to get it for *him*, and Dol coaxed me not. She said 'twant right; and, when I said I guessed God had liever he'd have it than Farmer Todd, she said, No: God gave it to Todd, and so he ought to have it. She was so set about it, I had to tell her I wouidn't take it."

"Such things show Dolly's true repentance and love to her Saviour," said Mrs. Bradford. "If we wish to please Jesus and come to Him, and are truly sorry for the wrong things we have done, we will try to undo them so far as we can."

She talked to Lem a little more of Dolly's new hope, and the Saviour's great love and forgiveness, and then told him they had better go on.

"Wonder what she wants these for, if she's goin' away to leave 'em," said Lem, sorrowfully, as he took up his flower-pots.

"Sick people often take such fancies," said Mrs. Bradford; "and when Dolly has gone you will be glad to think that you have pleased her by even such a small thing as caring for her plants."

"And I do think they've picked up a bit," said Lem. "See, this one has two buds on it. I wouldn't wonder if they made flowers."

When Mrs. Bradford and Lem reached the tool-house, or "Dolly's home," as the children now called it, they found the sick girl laid comfortably in the neat bed which had been provided for her; while Mrs. Rush and Mrs. Porter were beside her, feeding her with some nice beef-tea.

"Good Lem," she cried, when she saw the flower-pots; and then, turning to Mrs Porter, she asked, "Could you let them stay here?"

"To be sure, child," said Mrs. Porter; and Mrs. Bradford, taking the flower-pots from Lem, placed them in the little casement window opposite to Dolly's bed. Dolly looked pleased, but she was too much worn out to say more; and, when she had taken her tea, turned her face on her pillow, and fell into the most quiet sleep she had had since her illness.

XVII.

DOLLY GOES HOME.

DAY after day of the lovely September weather passed by, bringing change to God's world without and within. The days were warm and sunny, but the nights were cool; and now and then came the quiet frost, painting the grand old forest-trees and their clinging vines. The Virginia creepers — always the first to change — turned a bright crimson; here and there a maple flung out a scarlet branch, like a gorgeous banner in the air; while chestnuts and birch showed a few golden leaves, in beautiful contrast to the vivid green of the foliage which was yet untouched.

Each day Aunt Bessie improved. She came out among the family once more, and sat with them in hall, parlor, and piazza, and even took short drives and walks, though she was still pale, and the poor hurt arm could not yet be taken from the sling. But, as she said, she had now a dozen pairs of hands instead of one, for all were anxious to serve her, and could not do enough for the dear treasure they had so nearly lost.

But, though strength and health came to her with tender nursing and the lovely air and sunny days, they did not bring them to the poor little waif who had been cast upon the care and pity of these kind friends. She did not suffer much now, except when the cough racked her poor little wasted frame; but she grew weaker and weaker, and all knew that the end must soon come. Dolly had long been ailing, far more so than she imagined. Lem knew no more than herself, and there had been no one else to care for her. There had been no mother's quickened ear to mark the warning cough, no mother's loving eye to see the sunken cheek, no mother's tender hand to guard her child from damp and cold; and so the trouble had gone on unheeded and unchecked, till the night spent in the Ice Glen had finished the mischief already at work.

Maggie and Bessie came in to see her very often, bringing her fruit and flowers, and now and then some other little offering; some dainty which had been given to themselves and saved for her, a picture or a toy. For the toys she did not care much; indeed, they were so new to her that she scarcely understood them, and was too weak to play with them; but the pictures always interested her, especially one of Christ blessing little children, which Bessie had brought her. She would lie for hours with this in her hand, looking at it now and then with a pleased, happy smile, which said that it told its own story to her.

But as the poor little body grew weaker, her love and trust in her Saviour grew stronger and brighter. A very simple faith was that of poor Dolly; but she knew in whom she had trusted,— the Jesus who had died on the cross to save her soul and fit it for His heaven; and who had said, "Suffer little children to come unto me." And the "little one," as she called Bessie, had told her that Jesus meant *all* little children; that whoever would, might come to this blessed Saviour, and he would take them in His arms, and love and care for them. And Dolly "loved Him because he had first loved" her, and longed to go and live with Him for ever in that bright world where she had been told He waited for her.

It was wonderful to see how, without any direct teaching, she caught the words of the hymns the children sang to her, and how she would fit them to herself and her own needs.

As for Lem, he watched her with a sort of dumb sorrow which was touching to see. When he first saw Mr. Stanton, he made a piteous appeal to him, "to get her well, not to let her die;" and when the gentleman told him, as Mrs. Bradford had done, that he could do nothing, and that life and death were in the hands of God, who saw fit to take Dolly to Himself, he refused to speak or think of any thing for his own good

"Lem," said Dolly to him one day, "why don't you be glad I'm going to Jesus? I'm glad. I asked Him a many times to take me."

"'Cause I can't," said Lem, sullenly. "I thought we was goin' to get along fustrate if *he* looked after us; but 'taint no good gettin' to be engine driver now, if you're goin' away."

"Oh, yes, it is!" said Dolly; "and you'll be good, won't you, Lem, and not steal no more, and try to come to Jesus too; and I'll ask Him to help you like He helped me?"

"I don't see as it's much help to make you sick and let you die," said Lem.

"I don't know," said Dolly. "I guess, maybe it's just the bein' sick and dyin' is a good help. You know, Lem, if I hadn't a been sick and the little one found me there, I'd never a heard about Jesus, and I guess the best help He can give me is to take me right up there. I asked little one t'other day how she come in that out-of-the-way place, where I thought nobody never come 'cept for hidin', and she said the man brought her; but she thought

Jesus sent him, so she could tell me 'bout Him. I guess He did too; I guess He knew I was lonesome and tired, and would like to be an angel. Don't you think that was help, Lem; and wasn't He good to let it come to me?"

This had been said with many a pause and very feebly, for Dolly was too weak to talk much now; and a sudden fit of coughing took away her breath before Lem could answer.

The dying child had never lost her interest in the poor, sickly marigolds in her pots. They had for some reason, too, thrived rather better in their new home, and the two buds Lem had pointed out to Mrs. Bradford had grown larger, and one of them was now opening into a ragged, stunted flower. But it was very beautiful in poor Dolly's eyes, for she had raised and cared for it herself; and no other blossom could be so lovely for her. But the more she loved and cherished her own plant, the more bitterly did she grieve over the destruction of the gardens of the two little girls who had been so kind and forgiving to her. She knew for what purpose they had taken so much pains with them, especially with the heliotrope and geranium which had been so ruthlessly torn to pieces; for Mrs. Porter had told her, and her sorrow and repentance were very bitter and very sincere.

One Sunday morning, towards the end of September, Maggie and Bessie went over with their mother to see her. She was lying with her sunken eyes fixed on the marigolds, which stood on a small table beside the bed; and, oh, how wan, white, and wasted she looked! Yet there was a look of perfect peace on the poor face; and, when the children came in, she turned to them with a bright smile.

"They're coming on nice, aint they?" she said; "don't they look pretty?"

Maggie and Bessie were rather uncomfortable, for they did not think the forlorn marigolds pretty, and they did not wish to hurt Dolly's feelings by saying so; but mamma came to their relief, by saying, as she could with truth,—

"It has agreed with your pets to be up here, Dolly; they have done better since you came."

"Yes," said Dolly; and then asked, "Could you give me a nice bit of white paper and a scissor?"

"Certainly," said Mrs. Bradford, and sent Maggie over to the house for these things.

When Maggie came back, Dolly wanted to raise herself and take the things from her, but could not do it. Mrs. Bradford put her arm under the pillow and lifted her. Then the child tried to fold and cut the paper; but the trembling fingers had no power, and paper and scissors fell from them; while Dolly looked about her with a piteous, disappointed air.

"What is it you want, Dolly?" asked Mrs. Bradford; "cannot we do it for you?"

"I know," said Lem; "she wants to fix up her posy, like the gardener fixes 'em up to the big farm." Lem meant the homestead. "She seen him through the hedge, one day, doin' of it, and she said this mornin' she wanted hers fixed up that way."

Mrs. Bradford understood at once. Poor,

simple Dolly had seen the gardener shielding his choice blossoms by a circlet of fringed paper; and she would fain do as much for the stunted little favorite which was so lovely in her eyes.

"Maggie will cut it for you," said the lady; and, under her mother's direction, Maggie's deft little fingers soon prepared the paper to suit Dolly.

But she could not be satisfied without putting it about the flower with her own hands, while Lem held the pot for her; and it was touching to see how the poor, wasted fingers fluttered feebly about the blossom that was to outlive her,—touching it so tenderly, and folding the fringed paper about it with such care. It was done at last, and, as Mrs. Bradford laid her back, she looked at her work with a contented smile; and then, exhausted with the effort, closed her eyes, and whispered faintly, "Sing."

The little ones sang her favorite hymns, until she slept,—slept the last sleep which was to know an awakening upon earth,—and then stole softly out with their mother.

But mamma was back and forth all day,—far more so than usual; and in the afternoon, when the hour came for Sunday school, the children, knowing she was there, ran over to give her a kiss before they went to their class.

"We'll ask Dolly what she wants us to sing," said Maggie; "for you know she can hear us quite well from our Sunday bower."

The door stood open, for the day was so soft and warm, that, save for the changing leaves which showed that autumn was at hand, they might have thought themselves in midsummer. It was a lovely afternoon,—scarce a breath of air was stirring, and the lake lay calm and placid, the trees and rocks reflected on its surface with surprising clearness. A Sabbath hush was in the air; a kind of glory from the golden sunshine seemed to fall on all around,—on lake and mountain, woods and rocks, on the lawn and the cosy old house.

It streamed through the lattice of Dolly's little window too, and fell upon the small head which lay on the pillow. Mrs. Porter would have shut it out; but Dolly murmured, "No, no," and seemed to like it.

There was even a deeper stillness within the room than without, for there was an angel waiting there, and those who watched little Dolly felt his presence.

The children felt the solemn hush; and their little feet paused upon the threshold of the open door. Mamma and papa were there, Uncle Ruthven and Mrs. Porter; and poor Lem, crouched at Mr. Stanton's feet, his hands clasped about his knees, his head bent upon them.

Mamma put out her hand, and beckoned to the children; and, with careful steps, they came to the bedside.

"Would you like to speak to my little girls, Dolly?" asked Mrs. Bradford, gently.

Dolly opened her eyes, and fixed them on he children, with a wistful smile.

"You was good to Doll," she said, in a faint whisper. "Jesus sent you. He loves you, 'cause you was good — and — I'll be an angel — and tell Him — you teached me about Him, and — He'll love you more. Good-by."

"Good-by, Dolly," said Bessie, not knowing this was to be the last good-by, and yet with the tears gathering in her eyes.

"Good-by, Dolly," whispered Maggie; "we are going to our Sunday school, and you will hear us sing."

"We'll think a good deal about you, and sing all your hymns, shall we?" asked Bessie.

"Rest for the weary," sighed Dolly.

"My darlings," said mamma, "ask Aunt May to leave the lessons for this afternoon, and let you sing as long as you can;" and drawing them to her, she kissed first one, and then the other, with a long, tender kiss.

Dolly's eyes followed them, as they went out, and then came back to Mrs. Bradford's face with a longing, wistful look.

"What is it, my child?" asked the lady.

"I guess, if I'd had a mother, she'd kiss me, like that,— don't you?"

"Shall I kiss you, Dolly?" asked Mrs. Bradford, with tearful eyes.

"Could you?" said Dolly, with a brightening look.

Warm from the loving mother's heart came the motherly kiss, which Dolly had never known before; and with a long, satisfied sigh, she again closed her eyes.

Then came the sweet voices of the children and their teacher, hymn after hymn of infant praise floating in, as it seemed, on that soft, shimmering sunshine, and filling the little room with music. Dolly lay still, and they could not tell whether she were listening or not. Presently, she opened her eyes again, started, and murmured,—

"Oh! I don't want to go in the Ice Glen; it's dark and cold,"— then, more gently, " well, never mind; Jesus will take care of me, I guess,— yes, Jesus will. He'll let me — be an angel — to praise Him — day — and — night. He does — care — for me."

Slowly, slowly the words dropped from her lips; then came one or two fluttering sighs; and a little ransomed soul, thirsting for the water of life, had flown away, and was safe within the bosom of Him who has said, "Suffer little children to come unto me." The little, weary, homesick child had gone home to the love that never fails, to the care that never tires.

Lem came over to the Lake House, the next day, carrying one of Dolly's flower-pots on each arm; and, setting them down before Maggie and Bessie, who were on the piazza with Uncle Ruthven and Aunt Bessie, drew his sleeve across his eyes, and said,—

"She telled me I was to bring 'em to you, and say, maybe they'd go a little bit to make up for the sp'ilin' of your gardens, and maybe, when the flowers was out, they'd do to go to the show. That was what she was settin' so much by 'em for, when she lay a dyin'."

The tears which had not fallen over the happy little child who had gone to be an angel, fell fast over the simple tokens of gratitude and repentance she had left behind her; and faithful was the care bestowed upon them by our Maggie and Bessie.

Not with any thought of taking them to the flower show, however; it was only for Dolly's sake: it would never do to display these wretched little plants beside some of the really beautiful and flourishing things which their more fortunate brothers and cousins had raised. Besides, these were not of their own growing, and Maggie and Bessie had, long since, given up all thought of trying for a prize.

A few days after Dolly's death, Mrs. Bradford took up Maggie's second volume of " The Complete Family," which she had not looked over for some time, and there she found written something which touched her very much. Mingled with many other things, giving an account of their summer among the mountains, and written in Maggie's own droll, peculiar way, ran the story of Lem and Dolly, of their persecutions, and of the difficulty she and Bessie had had in forgiving their many injuries; but all that was not new to the mother, who now read for the first time what Maggie had written during the last week. It ran thus, leaving out Maggie's mistakes: —

"M. and B. Happy were very thankful to our Father in heaven, because he let them be of a mind to forgive Dolly. If they had not forgiven her, and made up their resolutions to do a kind thing for her, then B. would have run away when she saw Dolly, and not waited to speak to her and give the banana, and so nobody might have known that Dolly was sick, and she might have died without knowing about Jesus, who died for her; but she never knew it till Bessie told her. And, oh, how dreadful that would have been for M. and B. Happy! but God was so good as to spare them of it, and Dolly learned about Jesus, and loved Him, and wanted to please Him, only she did not have much time; but Jesus does not care about that, so long as she believed on Him, and loved Him, and He took Dolly away to His own heaven to live with Him. And M. and B. Happy were happy about it, even if Dolly was dead, because papa and mamma, and all our grown-up, wise people, think she is happy with Jesus; and we hope our Father will let it be a little jewel to carry to Him, when the angel takes us over the river, and the Elder Brother will say we did it unto Him, because we did it to His poor little lamb that did not know about Him. And now M. and B. Happy do not mind so much about the gardens, even though they can't try for a prize, and B. says she had rather have Dolly's little marigold than the prettiest prize that ever was, but I am afraid M. would not; but then, you see, she is not so very perfect as B., and besides I don't like the smell of the marigolds: I think it's awful. And God let M. have a very happy dream. M. knows it is foolish to think much about dreams, because they are not a bit of consequence, and she hopes any one who reads this will not think she was so foolish as to believe any thing about it; but it did make her feel a little glad about it, and B. liked it too. The dream was this: I was out by the lake with Bessie, but it was the night, and oh! there were so very many stars, and Dolly's little bed was out by the lake too, and she was in it, quite alive. And we heard voices all around, but we could not see where they came from; but we knew it was the angels, and they were calling to Dolly, and she came out of her bed, and tried to go, but she could not, because she had no wings. Then such a beautiful thing happened,— the stars came down out of the sky, and fixed themselves down to the ground where Dolly stood, and she went up, up, up on them, just as if they were steps, to heaven. And when she stepped over each one, it went right back to its place in the sky; but it left a long light behind it, like the shooting star we saw the other night; and at the top of the stair of stars was a soft, white cloud;

and when Dolly came to it, a hand came out of the cloud, and took her in, and we knew she was quite safe, and would never come back again. But for all I was glad M. cried, and dear mamma came and woke her up, and asked me why I cried, and kissed me, and I told her I was glad Dolly went to heaven, because she had no precious mamma to kiss and love her, or to tell her troubles and happinesses to. So it was a very happy, grateful thing, all about Dolly."

A very happy, grateful thing, the dear mamma thought it too; and very happy, grateful tears were those which dimmed her eyes as she read her little daughter's simple story, and then thanked God that the lessons of love and forgiveness which were given to her little ones fell not upon stony ground, but took root and bore precious fruit in those tender young hearts.

XVIII.

GOOD-BY TO CHALECOO.

AND now there was much talk of going home, and the time for the flower show was at hand, and our Maggie and Bessie could not help a little feeling of sorrow, that they had nothing to show that they had tried to do as well as the others. They had thought they should not mind it so very much; but as the time drew near, they found they did; and many a sigh and sad thought went to the memory of the lost heliotrope and geranium.

The day came, and the whole party from the Lake House, from grandmamma down to baby, were to go and spend the day at the homestead, and to have a grand family dinner after the flower show.

Soon after breakfast, the wagons came to the door, and the happy, merry party were ready to be packed in. The boys had already taken their seats in the last one, where the prize flowers and vegetables had been stored; and the little girls were waiting their time to be put snugly in between some of the older people, when Bessie suddenly bethought herself of the marigolds, which had not been attended to that morning.

"O Maggie!" she said: "we forgot to water Dolly's marigolds. Let's run and do it before we go."

Away they scampered to the side of the house where they had stood Dolly's treasures, but came back in a moment, with wondering faces, crying out,—

"Somebody has moved our marigolds."

"Where are our marigolds?"

"Never mind the marigolds now," said papa, catching up Bessie, and putting her into the wagon, where, the next moment, she was seated on Colonel Rush's knee,—"never mind the marigolds; they are safe, and will keep until you come back again;" and then he whisked Maggie into the wagon, and she was nestled into a seat beside Uncle Ruthven, with his arm about her to keep her from falling out.

Away they went, the whole party as merry as crickets, — laughing, singing, and joking, as they drove down the mountain. They might make as much noise as they pleased, on this lonely mountain road; there was no one, but the squirrels and the wood-pigeons to be consulted, and they did not seem to object to the fun. The woods were lovely to-day. Crimson and gold, scarlet and purple, were gaining fast upon the green of the past summer; each moment, some one was calling to the others to look here, and look there, at the brilliant leaves, so wonderful in the richness and variety of their gay coloring.

When they had come down into the valley, where farms and cottages lay, and where people were coming and going, papa said they had better make less noise, or these good, quiet folks would think them a band of wild Indians coming down from the mountains. But the boys were beside themselves with fun and frolic, and it seemed impossible for them to be quiet. They had a flag with them, which they waved and cheered whenever they passed a house or saw laborers at work in the fields; and the people seemed to like it, and came running to see the fun, and waved and cheered in return, as good-naturedly as if they thought it was all done for their pleasure.

As they passed Aunt Patty's cottage, she drove out of the gate in her low pony carriage, with Nonesuch before it, on their way to the homestead. The old lady nodded and smiled, as if she were glad to see them so happy, but Nonesuch seemed not only surprised, but displeased, at finding himself in such jolly company; and, after some shaking of his head and putting back of his ears, stood stock still in the middle of the road; nor could all Aunt Patty's coaxing or scolding, or even some gentle touches of the whip, persuade him to go on, till the whole party were out of sight. Aunt Patty and Nonesuch often had such differences of opinion, and I am sorry to say the donkey generally had the better of the old lady.

What a delightful bustle there was when our friends arrived at the homestead, and the whole family came pouring out to receive them! For the time, Maggie and Bessie forgot the little sore spot in their hearts which was caused by the thought that they had no share in that which brought them all together, until lisping little Katy Bradford, who was very fond of her young cousins, said,—

"Maggie and Bethie, I'm tho thorry you have no flowerth for the thow."

"Yes," said Bessie, "it's a very mournful thing for us; but we try not to think too much about it."

"Papa ith going to give very nith prithes," said Katy, taking a very poor way to console her cousins; but she meant well. "We think he ith going to give thome one a canary-bird. Thith morning there hath been a bird thinging — oh, tho thweetly! — in the libr'y where papa hath the pritheth, and will not let uth go in, and Aleck thaid it wath a canary."

Maggie gave a little sigh.

"Bessie and I want a canary very much," she said. "There is one in the nursery at home; but we want one for our own room, and we are going to ask mamma to let us have it next Christmas."

"I'd jutht like you to have thith one, 'cauthe you're tho good and I love you," said Katy, and she put up her lips, for a kiss, to first one little cousin and then the other.

And now Mr. Alexander Bradford said he should like to have papa, and Uncle Ruthven and the Colonel come with him, and act as judges on the fruit and flowers.

While the gentlemen were gone, making these last arrangements, the children had a good play; and in about an hour's time they were all called in to take part in the great event of the day. The spot chosen for this was the latticed piazza which served as the children's summer play-room; and here a long table was set out with the fruit, vegetables, and flowers, each of which it was hoped by the young owners might gain a prize.

The place looked very pretty. It was festooned with dahlias, chrysanthemums, and other bright-colored autumn flowers and leaves; and, although the display upon the table might not have seemed very grand to less interested eyes, the children desired nothing better; and it certainly did them great credit.

"Bessie," whispered Maggie, as they went in, "does it make you feel a little as if you was homesick for our geranium and heliotrope?"

"Yes," answered Bessie, in the same tone; "it makes the cry come in my throat, Maggie; but I am not going to let it come out, and I shall try to find enough of 'joyment in the others' 'joyment."

They kept very close together, these two

generous little girls, and hand in hand walked round the table to look at the pretty sight. Each article was labelled with its owner's name, and behind such as took a prize was the reward it was thought to have merited. Not a child but had some one pretty or useful gift; even the little Persian, who had not been very successful, but to whom Mr. Alexander Bradford had given a humming-top and ball, as the reward of his industry and perseverance.

Fred displayed an enormous melon which had been ripe for some days, and was now rather too mellow and soft, and, having been jolted somewhat severely on its ride down the mountain, had fallen to pieces, presenting, as joking Fred said, " a very *melon*choly sight." But Cousin Alexander had seen the melon in its glory, before it was taken from the vine; and, in spite of its present distressed appearance, Fred found a handsome six-bladed knife placed beside the fragments,—" A blade for each piece, and the handle thrown in," said pleased Fred; adding, that he thought Cousin

Alexander wanted an excuse for giving presents.

The little girls were standing lost in admiration of a miniature set of croquet, just the thing for small hands, and which had rewarded the care bestowed by Katy upon a lovely tea-rose, when Harry called suddenly from the other side of the room, —

"Hallo! Midget and Queen Bess, how came these old things here?" Then in a tone of still greater astonishment, "Why, I declare! Oh, what jolly good fun! Come here, pets, and see this!"

Maggie and Bessie ran round to the other side; and there, to their great surprise, stood Dolly's two marigolds. Forlorn enough they certainly looked among the flourishing plants and bright blossoms which had been the fruit of their cousins' labors; even more forlorn than they had done when Dolly left them as her dying legacy to the dear little ones who had been her friends.

The flower which had been in blossom when

she died, now hung black and withered on its feeble stem, kept there only by the fringed paper which she had put about it with such touching care. The second bud had half opened into another scragly, stunted flower, about which not even the most loving eyes could see the slightest beauty, and, in spite of the care which Maggie and Bessie had given them, the leaves of both plants were wilted and drooping. But there was more than one heart at that table for which those feeble, sickly plants had a value far beyond that of the richest and rarest exotic.

Beside the marigolds stood a bird-cage, and in it, hopping about, and with his little head perking from side to side, as he watched the scene so curious and new to him, was a beautiful canary-bird. He was not singing now, for he did not know what to make of it all, and was not quite sure whether he were pleased or no; but, as the children stood looking from him to the marigolds in blank amazement, he gave a little inquiring "cheep, cheep!" as a first move to a better acquaintance.

"Oh, the darling birdie!" cried Bessie; "who is he for?"

But Maggie exclaimed with a trembling lip, —

"Fred, Fred! it wasn't fair. You ought not to make fun of poor Dolly's marigolds, and to hurt our feelings that way."

"I did not do a thing," said Fred, "and knew no more about it than yourself."

"Nor I," said Harry: "most likely it was papa or some grown-up person; and certainly no one has meant to make fun of you. Don't you see the card on the cage, and what is written on it?"

Maggie looked at the card, as her brother moved the cage nearer to her.

"'For our Maggie and Bessie — the dear'— oh! what is it Harry? read it to me quick."

Harry read it, —

"For our Maggie and Bessie, the dear little workers in the garden of the Lord, who tended the Christian plants of patience, kindness, and forbearance, till their lovely blossoms overran the evil weeds of malice and ill-will, and sowed the seeds of that which brought forth fruit for the glory of God."

"I don't understand it," said Maggie. "Does it mean the canary is for Bessie and me?"

"Of course," said Harry.

"But I am sure we ought not to have any credit about the marigolds," said Maggie, still wondering. "If there is any, it is Dolly's or Lem's."

"And Harry," said Bessie, "the marigolds are pretty ugly. I don't much think we ought to have a prize, even if we had grown them up."

"Dolly left you the marigolds," said Harry; "so, if they win a prize you ought surely to have it, and I am glad of it, — that I am. But I don't quite think it was these poor little scrubs that had that honor."

"But, O Maggie! just to think of that lovely, darling, little birdie being for us," said Bessie, pleasure beginning to have its way over surprise; "and we never 'spected a thing 'cause we had no flowers."

"Yes," said Maggie, now in great delight as she began to understand how it was, "and we would rather have had it than any thing else."

Never was a birdie coaxed with more pretty names than was this one during the next ten minutes; and he seemed to like them well, for, after answering with one or two more half-timid "cheeps," he broke into a soft trill, which soon swelled into a clear, sweet song of joy.

Maggie and Bessie were in ecstasies, and Cousin Alexander certainly had reason to think his kindness had given all the pleasure he intended it should.

This was the last day they were to spend at the homestead, and the children made the most of it. Every nook and corner was visited, and all kinds of odd traps were dragged to light, and presented by the young cousins to be kept in memory of the old place, "family relics," Maggie called them; and very curious "family relics" some of them were. Among other things were two or three peacock feathers, a turkey wing, some pebbles from the brook where papa used to sail his boats when he was a boy, a piece of rusty tin pipe, which, because it looked black and smoky, and came from the field where the burnt barn had stood, they persuaded themselves must be a part of the very leader down which papa slid when he ran for the ladder to save his little brother, — all these, and other treasures of like value, were carefully collected and stowed in the wagons, to be carried to the Lake House, and thence to the city.

But at last the busy, happy day came to an end, and farewell had to be said to the dear old homestead and the kind family there.

Birdie did not like his ride up the mountain at all, but chirped in a very miserable, beseeching manner all the way; and, when he was safely at the Lake House and hung up out of the reach of Mrs. Porter's old pussy cat, tucked his head under his wing, and went to sleep at once, as if he were glad to forget all his troubles.

But he was bright enough the next morning; for he woke the little girls with his song some time before the hour at which they were accustomed to rise. Bessie, always a light sleeper, was the first to be roused by his sweet notes, that soft, half-doubtful little trill with which he began; but, as it rose into a gush of joyous music, Maggie, too, stirred, and opened her eyes. She listened a moment, then turned towards Bessie, who lay with her eyes fixed on the bird with a dreamy, thoughtful look.

"What are you thinking of, Bessie?" she asked, softly.

"I was thinking," said Bessie, "that it seemed as if our Father was letting the jewel of forgiveness sparkle a little for us here before we carried it over the river to Him."

"Yes," said Maggie, "I was thinking something like that last night, but I did not put it in such nice words; and I am just going to put in the Complete Family, that B. Happy said it. And perhaps, Bessie, if we had not taken up the jewel of prayer, and asked our

Father for help, we might never have found the other jewels."

"Or, if He had not helped us very much, we might not have taken them up, when we did find them," said Bessie. "It was pretty hard work to take up that first one of giving the banana to Dolly; and, Maggie, do you know I did such a very naughty thing as most to wish He did not give me the chance I had asked for: but, after that, all the rest were very easy to take up, and I did not find it at all hard to forgive Dolly every thing she had done."

"Yes," said Maggie: "I guess that's always the way, and after all, I did not have to forgive Lem and Dolly near so many times as 'seventy times seven.' Oh, yes, you darling birdie! do you want to say you know all about it? Bessie, let's think the canary is a kind of keepsake from Dolly, 'cause you know it seems as if it came by her, and mamma says it is of no use to take the marigolds to town, for they will be quite dead in a few weeks."

"Yes, so we will, Maggie, and that's a very

nice idea of you; and then we might call our birdie 'Marigold,' for memory of the poor little plants as well as Dolly."

"Oh, yes!" said Maggie; "that's lovely, so we just will."

So from this day the canary was called Marigold, nor was it long before he knew his name, and would answer with a chirp when it was called.

In two or three days more, they said good-by to Chalecoo and all its pleasures. The parting was a hard one on all sides, especially for Mr. Porter's family, who knew how much they would miss the sweet childish voices, the merry laughter, and patter of little feet, which had made the old house so gay and bright through all the long summer.

As for poor Lem, he was in despair. He had begged hard to go with Mr. Stanton, promising the best of behavior if he were only allowed to do so; but the gentleman did not think the city was the best place for a boy like Lem, and thought it wiser to leave him in the care of Mr. Porter, who promised to keep him for the winter, and give him work if he would try to do well, and be honest and industrious. In the spring, if Mr. Porter could give a good account of him, Mr. Stanton meant to send him out to sea, with some good, careful captain who would try to do well for the boy. Lem had such a fancy for a roving life, that this was thought the best thing for him; but just now even this promised pleasure was lost sight of in his grief at the loss of his kind friend. His father had never come back; and, from all that could be learned, it was believed that he had gone to a far-away country, leaving his poor children to shift for themselves.

All agreed that it was better so. A heavenly Father had cared for these poor desolate ones, and sent them help in the time of their greatest need. One had no longer need of earthly care, but was safe with Jesus in that home which He had bought for her with His precious blood; and for the other, there was much to be hoped. A strong desire to please

Mr. Stanton, and a fear of doing what would have grieved Dolly, kept him from much that was wrong; and he could scarcely be known for the same boy, who a few months since had been a terror to every small child and harmless animal, and a torment to every farmer and housekeeper in Chalecoo.

"Good-by! good-by! good-by!" The words, so hard to say, were spoken; and dear old Mrs. Porter stood upon the piazza steps, wiping her eyes with her apron, as she watched the wagons going slowly past the lake, and carrying our friends down the mountain for the last time.

"Well, I hope we may see them all back another summer," she said to Dolly and Fanny, who stood beside her, feeling almost as mournful; "if I'd known I'd feel so bad to part with them, I don't know as I could have made up my mind to take them: but those dear little ones have just taken the heart right out of me. Well, God bless them, wherever they may go."

"As He does," said Fanny, "for surely they

have brought a blessing here this summer. Who would have thought such little things could do a bit of good to those two?" and she looked at Lem, who lay with his face buried in the grass, trying to hide his tears; "and yet see what they've been the means of bringing to them."

"Ay, Fanny," said her mother, "little hands may do God's work, if they but take it up in His strength and with His help."

"Well," said Mr. Porter, when he had taken the homeward-bound party safely to the place where they were to take the boat down the river, "I reckon one of the best jobs I ever did was to take you up Chalecoo mountain for the first time, and one of the worst to bring you down for the last."

"But you can find *consolement* to think we are coming back some other time," said Maggie; "and we thank you very much for letting us have a nice time this summer, Mr. Porter."

"Yes," said Bessie, "we had a lovely, happy

time among the mountains, even if the sea was not there."

And now as we leave our Maggie and Bessie, are there not some little friends who will say that they have spent a useful as well as a happy summer among the mountains?

Cambridge: Press of John Wilson and Son.

530 Broadway, New-York.

ROBERT CARTER & BROTHERS'

NEW ✢ BOOKS.

NOBODY. A story by the author of the "Wide, Wide World." 12mo $1.75

"Her style is felicitous, her humor delicate, her pathos sincere. If we must have novels, commend us to such a story as "Nobody," which leaves in the lips of the reader a taste of sweetness, and upon his breath an odor of fragrance." —*Morning Star.*

UNIFORM WITH AND BY THE SAME AUTHOR.

1. **MY DESIRE.** A Story. 12mo $1.75
2. **THE END OF A COIL.** A Story. 12mo 1.75
3. **THE LETTER OF CREDIT.** A Story. 12mo 1.75

BY THE SAME AUTHOR.

The Say and Do Series. 6 vols. $7.50	Ellen Montgomery's Bookshelf.
Story of Small Beginnings. 4 vols 5.00	5 vols 5.00
King's People. 5 vols 7.00	THE OLD HELMET 2.25
Stories of Vinegar Hill. 3 vols.. 3.00	MELBOURNE HOUSE........... 2.00
	Pine Needles................... 1.50

Fifteen; or, Lydia's Happenings. By Mrs. Jennie M. Drinkwater Conklin. 12mo **1.50**

BY THE SAME AUTHOR.

Tessa Wadsworth's Discipline. 12mo $1.50	Rue's Helps. 12mo............ 1.50
	Electa. A Story. 12mo......... 1.50

Under the Shield. A Tale. By M. E. Winchester. 12mo. **1.50**

The Red and White. An Historical Tale. By Emily Sarah
  Holt. 12mo.. 1.50

At Ye Grene Griffin. By Emily Sarah Holt. 16mo..... 1.00

BY THE SAME AUTHOR.

Isoult Barry. 12mo............$1.50	Lettice Eden. 12mo............$1.50
Robin Tremayne. 12mo........ 1.50	For the Master's Sake. 16mo.... 1.00
The Well in the Desert. 16mo.. 1.25	Margery's Son. 12mo.......... 1.50
Ashcliffe Hall. 16mo........... 1.25	Lady Sybil's Choice. 12mo..... 1.50
Verena. A Tale. 12mo........ 1.50	The Maiden's Lodge. 12mo.... 1.25
The White Rose of Langley. 12mo 1.50	Earl Hubert's Daughter. 12mo.. 1.50
Imogen. 12mo................. 1.50	Joyce Morrell's Harvest. 12mo.. 1.50
Clare Avery. 12mo............ 1.50	

Decima's Promise. By Agnes Giberne................ 1.25

Twilight Talks; or, Early Lessons on Things about us.
  By Agnes Giberne. 16mo.............................. .75

Jacob Witherby; or, The Need of Patience. By Agnes
  Giberne. 16mo....................................... .60

BY THE SAME AUTHOR.

The World's Foundations; or, Geology for Beginners. Illus. 12mo...... 1.50
Sweetbriar; or, Doings in Priorsthorpe Manor. 12mo..................... 1.50
Through the Linn. 16mo.. 1.25

Aimee. A Tale of James II. 16mo. $1.50	Coulyng Castle. 16mo.......... 1.50
The Dwy Star; or, Gospel Stories. 1.25	Muriel Bertram. 16mo......... 1.50
The Curate's Home. 16mo..... 1.25	The Sun, Moon, and Stars. 12mo. 1.50
Floss Silverthorne. 16mo....... 1.25	Duties and Duties. 16mo....... 1.25

Nearer to Jesus. Memorials of Robert Walter Fergus.
  By his mother. With an introduction by Rev. J. Oswald
  Dykes, D. D... .75

Little Bullets and Seven Perils Passed by A. L. O. E.
  16mo. Illustrated..................................... 1.00

The Wondrous Sickle. By A. L. O. E. 16mo.......... .75

Cared For. By C. E. Bowen. 18mo................ .50

The Orphan Wanderers. Containing "Cared For" and "How a Farthing made a Fortune." Illus. 16mo....... 1.00

Heroic Adventure. Chapters in recent Exploration and Discovery. Illustrated. 12mo..........................

Only a Cousin. By Catharine Shaw..................... 1.25

Lonely Jack and his Friend. By Emily Brodie.......... 1.25

Seeketh Not Her Own. By M. Sitwell... .... 1.25

Cripple Jess, the Hop-Picker's Daughter............. 1.00

Jill and Jack. A Story of To-Day...................... 1.00

A Little Wild Flower................................ .60

Bennie, the King's Little Servant.................... .50

The Story of a Shell. By the Rev. J. R. Macduff, D. D.

Rex and Regina. By Mrs. Marshall................... 1.50

BY THE SAME AUTHOR.

Dew Drops and Diamonds......$1.50	The Primrose Series. 6 vols.... 3.00
Stories of Cathedral Cities........ 1.50	The Violet and Lily Series. 6 vols. 3.00
Ruby and Pearl 1.25	Chip of the Old Block........... .50
Framilode Hall.................. .50	Little Brothers and Sisters....... 1.25
Stellafont Abbey................. 1.00	Matthew Frost................. 1.00
Between the Cliffs.............. 1.00	

BITS FROM BLINKBONNY; or, Bell o' the Manse. 12mo. 6 illustrations................................... 1.50

THE CHURCH IN THE HOUSE; or, Lessons on Acts. New Edition. 12mo. (In Dec.)..................... 1.50

THE HUMAN MIND. A Treatise on Mental Philosophy. By Edward John Hamilton, D. D. 8vo................ 3.00

MOSES AND THE PROPHETS. A Review of Robertson Smith and Kuenen. By Professor Green, of Princeton. 12mo 1.50

GOD'S LIGHT ON DARK CLOUDS. By Theodore L. Cuyler, D. D. Very neat. Limp..................... .75

BY THE SAME AUTHOR.

FROM THE NILE TO NORWAY.. $1.50	THE EMPTY CRIB. 24mo. Gilt. 1.00
THOUGHT HIVES. With Portrait. 1.50	STRAY ARROWS. 18mo......... .60
POINTED PAPERS 12mo....... 1.50	CEDAR CHRISTIAN. 18mo...... .75

— ✤ —

HUGH MILLER'S WORKS.

The 12 volumes in 6. Neat cloth........................ 9.00

"Was there ever a more delightful style than that in which his works are written? His essays wed the elegance of Addison with the strength of Carlyle." —*Rev. Dr. W. M. Taylor.*

— ✤ —

GLEAMS FROM THE SICK CHAMBER. Macduff. .75

MANIFESTO OF THE KING. An Exposition of the Sermon on the Mount. By Rev. J. Oswald Dykes, D.D... 2.00

SERMONS. By J. Oswald Dykes, D. D. 12mo......... 1.50

COVENANT NAMES AND PRIVILEGES. A series of Discourses. By the Rev. Richard Newton, D. D. Portrait. 1.50

BY THE SAME AUTHOR.

The Jewel Case. 6 vols...................................... 7.50
The Wonder Case. 6 vols.................................... 7.50
Rays from the Sun of Righteousness 1.25
The King in His Beauty 1.25
Pebbles from the Brook 1.25

DAYSPRING. A Tale of the Time of Tyndale. Marshall $1.50

NOT FOR HIM. A Tale. By Emily Sarah Holt . . 1.25

BEK'S FIRST CORNER. Mrs. J. M. Drinkwater Conklin 1.50

THE GIANT-KILLER SERIES. By A. L. O. E. 10 vols. 16mo. In a box 8.50

Giant Killer and Sequel . .	$0.90	Lost Jewel	$0.90
Cyril Ashley	.90	Robber's Cave	.90
Giles Oldham	.90	Silver Keys	.90
Haunted Rooms	.90	Spanish Cavaliers	.90
Lady of Provence	.90	Try Again	.90

GOLDEN LIBRARY C. 10 vols. 16mo. In a box . $8.50

Brother's Watchword . . .	$0.90	Jamie Gordon	$0.90
Clara Stanley	.90	Mabel's Experience . . .	.90
Days at Muirhead	.90	Mia and Charlie	.90
Ellie Randolph	.90	Rival Kings	.90
Happy Home	.90	Sidney Grey	.90

TOWARDS THE SUNSET. By the Author of the "Recreations of a Country Parson" $1.00

THE CHRISTIAN SCRIPTURES: Their Claims, History, and Authority. By Professor Charteris . . . 2.00

THE PROGRESS OF DOCTRINE IN THE NEW TESTAMENT. By Bernard. 12mo 1.25

*****D'AUBIGNE'S REFORMATION IN THE SIXTEENTH CENTURY.** 5 vols. in one. 8vo 1.00

KRUMMACHER'S SUFFERING SAVIOUR. 12mo 1.00

MACDUFF'S SUNSETS ON THE HEBREW MOUNTAINS. 12mo 1.00

MACDUFF'S FAMILY PRAYERS. 16mo. Reduced to 1.00

PRIME'S FORTY YEARS IN THE TURKISH EMPIRE. Life of Goodell. 12mo 1.50

DOROTHY COPE. Containing the "Old Looking-Glass" and the "Broken Looking-Glass." By Miss Charlesworth. 12mo 1.50

The Claremont Series. By A. L. O. E. 10 vols. 16mo.
In a box... 8.50

Eddie Ellerslie...........$0.90	Christian's Panoply......$0.90
Claremont Tales........... .90	Cortley Hall.............. .90
Christian's Mirror......... .90	Idols in the Heart........ .90
Crown of Success......... .90	Needle and Rat............ .90
Christian Conquests....... .90	Stories on Parables....... .90

The Golden Library, A. 10 vols. 16mo............... 8.50

The Golden Library, B. 10 vols. 16mo............... 8.50

*THE OLIVE LIBRARY. 40 vols. 16mo. Wooden
Case. Net 25.00

— ✠ —

A MARVEL OF CHEAPNESS.

DR. HANNA'S LIFE OF CHRIST.

Pica type, fine paper, 3 vols. 12mo, 2182 pp., neat cloth...... 2.50

— ✠ —

New and Very Neat Editions of

MIND AND WORDS OF JESUS.

By Macduff. Limp, red edges, 50 cents. Gilt edges, 60 cents. Superfine paper, *red line* edition, round corners, gilt edges, $1.00. In full calf, gilt edges, $2.50.

MORNING AND NIGHT WATCHES.

By Macduff. Limp, red edges, 50 cents. Gilt edges, 60 cents. Superfine paper, *red line* edition, round corners, gilt edges, $1.00. In full calf, gilt edges, $2.50.

MIND AND WORDS AND MORNING AND NIGHT WATCHES. In One Volume.

Red line edition, gilt edges, $1.50. Full calf, gilt edges, $3.50.

HANNAH MORE'S PRIVATE DEVOTION.

32mo. Limp, red edges, 50 cents. Gilt edges, 60 cents.

DICKSON (REV. ALEXANDER, D. D.)

ALL ABOUT JESUS................................. 2.00
BEAUTY FOR ASHES............................... 2.00

"His book is a 'bundle of myrrh,' and will be specially enjoyed by those who are in trouble."—*Rev. Dr. W. M. Taylor.*

"Luscious as a honeycomb with sweetness drawn from God's word."—*Rev. Dr. Cuyler.*

THE BEST COMMENTARY.

*MATTHEW HENRY'S COMMENTARY ON THE BIBLE. 5 vols., quarto, sheep, $20.00. In cloth 15.00
Another edition, 9 volumes, 8vo, cloth.................. 20.00

Rev. C. H. Spurgeon says: "First among the mighty for general usefulness we are bound to mention the man whose name is a household word— MATTHEW HENRY."

Rev. Dr. Wm. M. Taylor says: "Among the valuable homiletical commentaries is Matthew Henry's, which sparkles with jewels of wisdom and incisive humor."

Rev. T. L. Cuyler, D. D., says: "Next to wife and children has lain near the minister's heart the pored-over and prayed-over copy of his Matthew Henry, king of all Bible explorers yet."

Rev. Dr. Archibald Alexander says: "Taking it as a whole, and as adapted to every class of readers, this Commentary may be said to combine more excellence than any other work of the kind that was ever written in any language."

GUIDE TO FAMILY DEVOTION. By the Rev. Alexander Fletcher, D. D. Royal quarto, with 10 steel plates (half morocco, $7.50; Turkey morocco, $12), cloth, gilt, and gilt edges, $5.00.

"The more we look over the volume the more we admire it, and the more heartily feel to commend it to families and devout Christians. It is emphatically a book of devotion, from the standpoint of an intelligent, broad-minded Christian minister, who has here expressed many of the deepest emotions and wants of the soul. The selections of Scripture and the hymns are all admirably adapted to increase devotion; and the prayers are such as can but aid the suppliant, even when not uttered from his precise standpoint, and are especially valuable to many heads of families who find it difficult to frame words for themselves in conducting family worship."—*Journal and Messenger.*

RYLE ON THE GOSPELS. 7 vols., 12mo 10.50
Matthew, $1.50. *Mark,* $1.50. *Luke,* 2 vols., $3.00. *John,* 3 vols., $4.50.

"Those who are engaged in teaching others will find in them a treasury, full of edifying and instructive suggestions."— *Episcopal Register.*

KITTO'S BIBLE ILLUSTRATIONS. 8 vols., 12mo, in a box, with complete index.......................... 7.00

"I cannot lose this opportunity of recommending, in the strongest language and most emphatic manner I can command, this invaluable series of books. I believe for the elucidation of the historic parts of Scripture, there is nothing comparable with them in the English or any other language."—*J. A. James.*

DR. HODGE'S COMMENTARIES. 4 vols......... 7.00

Corinthians, 2 vols., $3.50. *Romans*, $1.75. *Ephesians*, $1.75.

"Dr. HODGE's Commentaries ought to be in the hands of all readers of the Bible, in families, in Sabbath-schools and Seminaries."—*Observer.*

HODGE'S (DR. A. A.) OUTLINES OF THEOLOGY. 8vo... 3.00

* **DR. McCOSH'S WORKS.** 5 vols., 8vo, uniform. Brown cloth 10.00

* **MURDOCK'S MOSHEIM'S ECCLESIASTICAL HISTORY.** 3 vols. in one......................... 3.00

* **POOL'S ANNOTATIONS UPON THE HOLY BIBLE.** 3 vols., 8vo................................ 7.50

* **THE WORKS OF PRESIDENT EDWARDS.** 4 vols., 8vo... 6.00

THE BOOK OF JOB. Illustrated. With fifty engravings after drawings by JOHN GILBERT. In morocco, $7.50; half calf, $6.00; cloth, gilt............................ 4.50

COWPER'S TASK. Illustrated. With sixty superb designs by BIRKET FOSTER. Printed on fine tinted paper; elegantly bound in cloth, gilt.......................... 3.50

GRAY'S ELEGY. Illustrated pocket edition. Gilt edges. .50

VOICES OF HOPE AND GLADNESS. By RAY PALMER, D. D. Illustrated. 12mo, gilt 1.50

SONGS OF THE SOUL. By Dr. PRIME. Quarto, gilt. 5.00
Cheaper edition, 12mo.....$2.00.

Recent Juveniles.

— ✠ —

Alice Neville.................. $1.25	Home Lessons..... .... $1.25
Between the Cliffs 1.00	Hosannas of the Children....... 1.50
Bible Echoes. *Wells*........... 1.25	House in the Glen............. 1.25
Bible Children. *Wells*.......... 1.25	Indian Stories.................. .75
Bible Images. 12mo. *Wells*.. 1.25	Interpreter's House. 16mo..... 1.25
Blackberry Jam. *Mathews*..... 1.25	Jack o' Lantern 1.25
Bobby and Rosie. 16mo........ 1.00	Jean Lindsay. *Brodie*.......... 1.25
Bread and Oranges............. 1.25	Katy and Jim. *Mathews*....... 1.25
Brentford Parsonage............ 1.25	Leaders of Men. *Page*. 12mo.. 1.50
Brighter than the Sun........... 2.00	Little Brothers and Sisters...... 1.2
Broken Mallet. *Mathews*...... 1.25	Little Friends at Glenwood...... 1.25
Broken Walls. *Warner*........ 1.25	Little Lights along Shore........ 1.25
Captivity of Judah.............. .60	Little Maid. *A. L. O. E.*...... .75
Christie's Old Organ............ .50	Little Mother Mattie 1.25
Christie's Organ, Saved at Sea, and Little Faith. 16mo....... 1.00	Little and Wise. 16mo......... 1.25
	Lyon's Den; or, Boys will be Boys 1.50
Comfort Strong................. 1.25	Mabel Hazard................... 1.25
Doors Outward................. 1.25	Mabel's Stepmother. 16mo..... 1.25
Duties and Duties. *Agnes Giberne* 1.25	Mabel Walton.................. 1.25
Eden in England .... .75	Maggie's Mistake 1.25
Eleanor's Visit. *Mathews*...... 1.25	Master Missionaries. *Japp*..... 1.50
Ella's Half Sovereign............ 1.25	Milly's Whims 1.25
Elsie's Santa Claus 1.25	Moore's Forge.................. 1.25
Fan's Brother. *Beatrice Marshall* .50	Nellie's Secret.................. 1.00
Fighting the Foe 1.50	New Scholars 1.25
Flag of Truce. *Warner*........ 1.25	Odd One, The.................. 1.25
Footsteps of St. Peter........... 2.00	Olive's Story. 16mo........... .75
Fred and Jeanie................. 1.25	Our Captain; or Heroes of Barton School 1.25
Fritz's Victory................... .50	
Gabled Farm.................... 1.25	Oliver of the Mill............... 1.50
Giant-Killer and Sequel......... 1.25	Palace Beautiful................ 1.25
Giants and Wonders 1.25	Peep Behind the Scenes......... 1.00
Giuseppe's Home 1.10	Reef. *Bickersteth* 1.25
Gold Thread .... .75	Rob and Mag. 16mo........... .75
Golden Fleece................... .75	Rosalie's Pet.................... 1.25
Grandmamma's Recollections.... 1.25	Rose Dunbar's Mistake 1.50
Haunted Rooms................. .75	Sword of De Bardwell. *Phipps*.. 1.00
Hebrew Heroes.................. .75	Uncle Fred's Shilling............ 1.25
Helen Hervey's Change.......... .75	Uncle Joe's Thanksgiving....... 1.25
Heroism of Christian Women.... 1.50	Victory Stories.................. .75
Hero in the Battle............... .50	Was I Right? *Walton*......... 1.00
Hilda; or, Seeketh not Her Own. 1.25	Wicket Gate. 16mo............ 1.25
His Grandchild.................. 1.00	Wise Words and Loving Deeds.. 1.50

SETS IN BOXES.

The Jewel Case. 6 vols.......$7.50	Stories of Small Beginnings. 4 vols.......................... 5.00
The Wonder Case. 6 vols..... 7.50	Ministering Children Library. 4 vols.......................... 3.00
Win and Wear Series. 6 vols.. 7.50	Little Kitty's Library. 6 vols.. 3.00
Green Mountain Stories. 5 vols. 6.00	Harry and Dolly Library. 6 vols. 3.00
Ledgeside Series. 6 vols...... 7.50	Rainbow Series. 5 vols....... 3.00
Butterfly's Flights. 3 vols.... 2.25	Primrose Series. 6 vols....... 3.00
The Bessie Books. 6 vols..... 7.50	Peep of Day Library. 8 vols... 4.50
The Flowerets. 6 vols......... 3.60	Drayton Hall Series. 6 vols... 4.50
Little Sunbeams. 6 vols....... 6.00	Golden Ladder Series. 3 vols.. 3.00
Kitty and Lulu Books. 6 vols.. 3.60	Dare to Do Right Series. 5 vols........................ 5.50
Miss Ashton's Girls. 6 vols.... 7.50	Tales of Christian Life. 5 vols. 5.00
Haps and Mishaps. 6 vols...... 7.50	Tales of Many Lands. 5 vols... 5.00
Heroes of Israel. 5 vols....... 5.00	Springdale Series. 6 vols..... 2.00
The King's People. 5 vols..... 7.00	The Great and Good. 4 vols... 6.00
Highland Series. 6 vols....... 7.50	Violet and Lily Series. 6 vols. 3.00
Ellen Montgomery's Bookshelf. 5 vols.......................... 5.00	Golden Library, A. 10 vols.... 8.50
Stories of Vinegar Hill. 3 vols. 3.00	Golden Library, B. 10 vols.... 8.50
The Say and Do Series. 6 vols. 7.50	
Claremont Series. 10 vols..... 8.50	

The A. L. O. E. Library. In 55 vols. 18mo. In a neat wooden case 40.00

"All these stories have the charm and pure Christian character, which have made the name of A. L. O. E. dear to thousands of homes."—*Lutheran.*
"The writings of this author have become a standard, and the mystic imprint, A. L. O. E., is ample assurance that the truth of the Gospel is beneath."—*Episcopalian.*

— ✠ —

OLD FAVORITES.

The Bessie Books. By Joanna H. Mathews. Fancy cloth. Chromo on cover. 6 vols. 16mo...................... 7.50

BY THE SAME AUTHOR.

The Flowerets. 6 vols. 18mo..$3.60	Kitty and Lulu Books. 6 vols. 18mo............. .... 3.60
Little Sunbeams. 6 vols. 16mo. 6.00	
Haps and Mishaps. 6 vols. 16mo. 7.50	Miss Ashton's Girls. 6 vols. 16mo. 7.50

Ministering Children and Sequel. 2 vols. 12mo. Each. 1.50

Oliver of the Mill. By the same author. 12mo.......... 1.50

The Peep of Day Library; or, Bible History for Very Little Children. With 90 full-page illustrations. 8 vols. 18mo.. 4.50

Mamma's Bible Stories and Sequel. New edition. Chromo on side. Each................................... .75

Very Little Tales for Very Little Children. New edition. Two vols. in one. Chromo on side............. .75

Little Annie's First and Second Books. In one vol. Chromo on side.. .75

SPURGEON'S WORKS.

A NEW, NEAT, AND VERY CHEAP EDITION OF

SPURGEON'S SERMONS,

COMPRISING NEARLY TWO HUNDRED AND FIFTY DISCOURSES,
WITH COMPLETE INDEXES OF BOTH TEXTS AND SUBJECTS.

10 vols. 12mo. $10.00.

THE VOLUMES ARE SOLD SEPARATELY, VIZ.:—

FIRST SERIES.	$1.00
SECOND SERIES.	1.00
THIRD SERIES	1.00
FOURTH SERIES	1.00
FIFTH SERIES	1.00
SIXTH SERIES	1.00
SEVENTH SERIES	1.00
EIGHTH SERIES	1.00
NINTH SERIES	1.00
TENTH SERIES	1.00

SPURGEON'S OTHER WORKS.

MORNING BY MORNING.	$1.00
EVENING BY EVENING	1.00
TYPES AND EMBLEMS	1.00
SAINT AND SAVIOUR	1.00
FEATHERS FOR ARROWS.	1.00
LECTURES TO STUDENTS	1.00
COMMENTING AND COMMENTARIES	1.00
JOHN PLOUGHMAN'S TALK	.75
GLEANINGS AMONG SHEAVES	.60
SPURGEON'S GEMS	1.00

From an Editorial Note to Volume Ten, by the Rev. JOHN STANFORD HOLME, D.D.

"If there is a minister of the gospel in the world who is truly cosmopolitan, that man is Charles H. Spurgeon. Mr. Spurgeon has now ministered for many years to the largest congregation in the world. To see him and to hear him has become a matter of curiosity to all who visit the great metropolis. But it is not on these accounts chiefly that he is a man of general interest throughout Christendom. It is rather that over fifteen hundred of the sermons of this one man have been accurately reported and printed. It is that the number of readers of these sermons has continued steadily to increase for more than twenty years, until now they are read weekly by hundreds of thousands wherever the English tongue is spoken. It is, above all, that these sermons have been blessed to the conversion and edification of multitudes in all lands.

"Many of the causes of the wonderful popularity of this distinguished preacher are not difficult to discover. In freshness and vigor of thought, in simplicity and purity of language, in grasp of gospel truth, and in tact and force in its presentation, he is perhaps without a peer in the pulpit. . . .

"It is not his manner to spin his web out of himself. The resources from which he draws are not measured by the strength and the store of his own faculties, but rather by the infinite fulness of the divine word. He never preaches from a topic. He always has a text. His text is not a mere motto, but in it he finds his sermon. He uses his text with as much reverence and appreciation as if those few words were the only words God had ever spoken. The text is the germ which furnishes the life, — the spirit and substance of the discourse. Every sermon has the peculiar flavor and fragrance and color of the divine seed-truth of which it is the growth.

"It is not surprising, therefore, that sermons so varied, fresh, and evangelical, should have so large a circulation. . . . As some of these volumes have had an issue of one hundred thousand copies, it will be seen that the circulation of these sermons even in this country is altogether without precedent; and, as the verdict of the Christian public, it fully justifies the estimate we have placed upon them."

www.ingramcontent.com/pod-product-compliance
Lightning Source LLC
Chambersburg PA
CBHW020243240426
43672CB00006B/619